# Prepare for the Great Tribulation and the Era of Peace

To Stacey

May the peace & grace of
Jesus be with you always

John Leary

D0967329

# Prepare for the Great Tribulation and the Era of Peace

## Volume XI:
## April 1, 1998 – June 30, 1998

by John Leary

**PUBLISHING COMPANY**
P.O. Box 42028 Santa Barbara, CA 93140-2028
(800) 647-9882 • (805) 957-4893 • Fax: (805) 957-1631

The publisher recognizes and accepts that the final authority regarding these apparitions and messages rests with the Holy See of Rome, to whose judgement we willingly submit.

– The Publisher

Cover art by Josyp Terelya

©1998 Queenship Publishing

Library of Congress Number # 95-73237

Published by:
    Queenship Publishing
    P.O. Box 42028
    Santa Barbara, CA 93140-2028
    (800) 647-9882 • (805) 957-4893 • Fax: (805) 957-1631

Printed in the United States of America

ISBN: 1-57918-096-5

# Acknowledgments

It is in a spirit of deep gratitude that I would like to acknowledge first the Holy Trinity: Father, Jesus, and the Holy Spirit, the Blessed Virgin Mary and the many saints and angels who have made this book possible.

My wife, Carol, has been an invaluable partner. Her complete support of faith and prayers has allowed us to work as a team. This was especially true in the many hours of indexing and proofing of the manuscript. All of our family has been a source of care and support.

I am greatly indebted to Josyp Terelya for his very gracious offer to provide the art work for this publication. He has spent three months of work and prayer to provide us with a selection of many original pictures. He wanted very much to enhance the visions and messages with these beautiful and provocative works. You will experience some of them throughout these volumes.

A very special thank you goes to my spiritual director, Fr. Leo J. Klem, C.S.B. No matter what hour I called him, he was always there with his confident wisdom, guidance and discernment. His love, humility, deep faith and trust are a true inspiration.

My appreciation also goes to Father John V. Rosse, my good pastor who is retiring from Holy Name of Jesus Church. He has been open, loving and supportive from the very beginning.

There are many friends and relatives whose interest, love and prayerful support have been a real gift from God. Our own Wednesday, Monday and First Saturday prayer groups deserve a special thank you for their loyalty and faithfulness.

Finally, I would like to thank Bob and Claire Schaefer of Queenship Publishing for providing the opportunity to bring this message of preparation, love and warnings to you the people of God.

John Leary, Jr.

# Dedication

To the Most Holy Trinity

God

The Father, Son and Holy Spirit

The Source of

All

Life, Love and Wisdom

# Publisher's Foreword

John has, with some exceptions, been having visions twice a day since they began in July, 1993. The first vision of the day usually takes place during morning Mass, immediately after he receives the Eucharist. If the name of the church is not mentioned, it is a local Rochester, NY, church. When out of town, the church name is included in the text. The second vision occurs in the evening, either at Perpetual Adoration or at the prayer group that is held at Holy Name of Jesus Church.

Various names appear in the text. Most of the time, the names appear only once or twice. Their identity is not important to the message and their reason for being in the text is evident. First names have been used, when requested by the individual.

We are grateful to Josyp Terelya for the cover art, as well as for the art throughout the book. Josyp is a well-known visionary and also, the author of *Witness* and most recently *In the Kingdom of the Spirit*.

This volume covers messages from April 1, 1998 through June 30, 1998. The volumes will now be coming out quarterly due to the urgency of the messages.

Volume I: July, 1993 through June, 1994.
Volume II: July, 1994 through June, 1995.
Volume III: July, 1995 through July 10, 1996.
Volume IV: July 11, 1996 through September 30, 1996.
Volume V: October 1, 1996 through December 31, 1996.
Volume VI: January 1, 1997 through March 31, 1997.
Volume VII: April 1, 1997 through June 30, 1997.
Volume VIII: July 1, 1997 through September 30, 1997.
Volume IX: October 1, 1997 through December 31, 1997.
Volume X: January 1, 1998 through March 31, 1998.

The Publisher

# Foreword

It was in July of 1993 that Almighty God, especially through Jesus, His Eternal Word, entered the life of John Leary in a most remarkable way. John is 55 years old and is a retired chemist from Eastman Kodak Co., Rochester, New York. He lives in a modest house in the suburbs of Rochester with Carol, his wife of thirty-two years, and Catherine, his youngest daughter. His other two daughters, Jeanette and Donna, are married and have homes of their own. John has been going to daily Mass since he was seventeen and has been conducting a weekly prayer group in his own home for twenty-five years. For a long time, he has been saying fifteen decades of the Rosary each day.

In April of 1993 he and his wife made a pilgrimage to Our Lady's shrine in Medjugorje, Yugoslavia. While there, he felt a special attraction to Jesus in the Blessed Sacrament. There he became aware that the Lord Jesus was asking him to change his way of life and to make Him his first priority. A month later in his home, Our Lord spoke to him and asked if he would give over his will to Him to bring about a very special mission. Without knowing clearly to what he was consenting, John, strong in faith and trust, agreed to all the Lord would ask.

On July 21, 1993 the Lord gave him an inkling of what would be involved in this new calling. He was returning home from Toronto in Canada where he had listened to a talk of Maria Esperanza (a visionary from Betania, Venezuela) and had visited Josyp Terelya. While in bed, he had a mysterious interior vision of a newspaper headline that spelled "DISASTER." Thus began a series of daily and often twice daily interior visions along with messages, mostly from Jesus. Other messages were from God the Father, the Holy Spirit, the Blessed Virgin Mary, his guardian angel and many of the saints, especially St. Therese of Lisieux. These messages he recorded on his word processor. In the beginning, they were quite short, but they became more extensive as the weeks passed by. At the time of this writing, he is still receiving visions and messages.

These daily spiritual experiences, which occur most often immediately following Communion, consist of a brief vision which becomes the basis of the message that follows. They range widely on a great variety of subjects, but one might group them under the following categories: warnings, teachings and love messages. Occasionally, there are personal confirmations of some special requests that he made to the Lord.

The interior visions contain an amazing number of different pictures, some quite startling, which hardly repeat themselves. In regard to the explicit messages that are inspired by each vision, they contain deep insights into the kind of relationship God wishes to establish with His human creatures. There, also, is an awareness of how much He loves us and yearns for our response. As a great saint once wrote: "Love is repaid only by love." On the other hand, God is not a fool to be treated lightly. In fact, did not Jesus once say something about not casting pearls before the swine? Thus, there are certain warnings addressed to those who shrug God off as if He did not exist or is not important in human life.

Along with such warnings, we become more conscious of the reality of Satan and the forces of evil "...which wander through the world seeking the ruin of souls." We used to recite this at the end of each low Mass. In His love and concern for us, Our Lord keeps constantly pointing out how frail we humans are in the face of such evil angelic powers. God is speaking of the necessity of daily prayer, of personal penance, and of turning away from atheistic and material enticements which are so much a part of our modern environment.

Perhaps the most controversial parts of the messages are those which deal with what we commonly call Apocalyptic. Unusual as these may be, in my judgment, they are not basically any different than what we find in the last book of the New Testament or in some of the writings of St. Paul. After a careful and prayerful reading of the hundreds of pages in this book, I have not found anything contrary to the authentic teaching authority of the Roman Catholic Church.

The 16th Century Spanish mystic, St. John of the Cross, gives us sound guidelines for discerning the authenticity of this sort of phenomena involving visions, locutions, etc. According to him, there are three possible sources: the devil, some kind of self-imposed hypnosis or God. I have been John's spiritual confidant for over five years. I have tested him in various spiritual ways and I am most confident that all he has put into these messages is neither of the devil nor of some kind of mental illness. Rather, they are from the God who, in His love for us, wishes to reveal His own Divine mind and heart. He has used John for this. I know that John is quite ready to abide by any decision of proper ecclesiastical authority on what he has written in this book.

Rev. Leo J. Klem, C.S.B.
Rochester, New York
1993

# Visions and Messages of John Leary:

**Wednesday, April 1, 1998:**
After Communion, I could see a small boat in the water. Then I saw a light of a spirit body rise up out of the water. Jesus said: **"My people, while you are here on earth, I offer My hand to lead you through life as a boat is needed to cross the water. Many of My children do not want to take My hand, but they try to struggle through life on their own. You are placed on this earth to know, love, and serve Me as the angels do. This life is a testing time for you to learn how to follow My Will for you. Those, who refuse to love Me or acknowledge Me, are the lost sinners that I seek to save. These are the ones I ask of you to throw life preservers to, so you can bring them back to Me. At the end of your lives, you are seeing the spirit bodies being called before Me. Your souls live on to face your judgment. Those, who are faithful, I will bring to Heaven. Those, who refuse to accept Me, will face eternity in Hell. Then on the day of the final judgment, My faithful will be resurrected with their glorified bodies. This will be a celebration of Easter Sunday which My faithful will enjoy and be eternally grateful."**

**Thursday, April 2, 1998:**
After Communion, I could see some large dark speakers. Jesus said: **"My son, I am calling you to continually speak out the messages that I have given you. Do not hold back, but go where you are able to share My love and peace. Some of the warning messages are difficult for some to hear, but it is more important that they be known. Your time for distributing the messages grows short, before these events will start. Once the Anti-**

*"This is My Divine Son, listen to Him."*

christ and his agents gain power, you will be prevented from speaking further. So it is with all of My faithful as well. I call on all those baptized and eager to spread My Gospel, to go forward now and evangelize the lost sinners. Time is growing short to bring these sinners around. Call on My help and that of the angels to spread the Gospel message. Satan and his minions will make it difficult for you to touch these hearts as all kinds of roadblocks and distractions will be thrown before you."

Later, at the prayer group, I saw a night scene and there was a green bush being blown around in the wind. I then saw a large tall tree and light was coming from it. Jesus said: **"My people, you are like the bush which gets blown around by the trials of life. Look to Me, who died on the tree of the Cross, which stands firm as your means to salvation. Come to Me for safety and assurance of My love to strengthen you in your trials. With Me leading you, why should you have any fear?"**

I could see some tents for the Holy of Holies. Then there was a vision of the Transfiguration of Jesus with God the Father above Him with Moses and Elijah. God the Father spoke: **"I AM hears your request for this picture that you desire. Let it represent Me as witnessing to the glory of My Divine Son with Moses and Elijah present. I said then as I say now 'This is My Divine Son, listen to Him.' My Son has revealed to you in His own words how We are One and that He does everything according to My Word. Follow the words of Jesus in the Scriptures and the messages that He gives."**

(Note: We dedicated our prayer group to the Eternal Father and we were praying for His desire for a painting to be done for it.)

I could see a statue of Mary sitting on a glass stand with oil all over it. Mary said: **"My dear children, your mother is crying tears of love for all of you. These statues, that are tearing in various ways, are a sign to you of my sorrow for all that you are doing to offend my Son, Jesus. See this as a sign that you need to reform your lives, especially this Lent. Heaven is showing you many signs to confirm my messages, but few are praying as I have asked you."**

I could see a king who turned everything into gold as King Midas. Jesus said: **"My people, many seek money enough to secure their lives. Those, who love money, are never satisfied with a sufficient amount to survive. They desire more amd more without limit. Do not seek to be rich for yourselves. You need to share all that you have with others. If you seek the Kingdom of God first, all that you need will be given you. So do not let riches control you, for they will be lost tomorrow."**

I could see some small ore cars being brought out of a mine that was being run by slave labor. Jesus said: **"My people, this is** the future trial that those, who believe in Me, will have to suffer. Some of My followers will be martyred, some enslaved to the Antichrist, and others will be protected in hiding. For those, who refuse to believe in My messages of hiding, this will be your fate, if you refuse the Mark of the Beast. Pray for understanding, so many of My faithful will be spared this severe persecution for believing in My Name."

I could see a man turning a key in an electrical device and a large picture screen came alive with the Antichrist speaking to his subjects. Jesus said: "**My people, do not sell your soul for worshiping the Antichrist and taking his mark. You are to avoid anyone who claims to be Me. His power of persuasion will overpower you, if you do not have My power with you. Pray your Rosaries and keep your Blessed Sacramentals with you and you will be spared. Those, who refuse to love Me and seek My help, will be drawn to serve the Antichrist over Me. Without My help, you will be lost. So seek My protection and everything will be provided for you.**"

I could see Jesus suffering on the cross and there was an open wrist watch nearby. Jesus said: "**My people, I am appealing to you from My suffering on the Cross. You do not realize how little time you have before your own cross will be coming with the tribulation about to begin. Do not be comfortable in your pleasures and rich houses, but use this grace of time for prayer, fasting, and meditation on your sins. Seek to have your sins forgiven in Confession and pray as if each day was your last day. In this way you will be spiritually prepared as the wise virgins. So when the Bridegroom comes, you will have oil in your lamps and you will be ready to meet Me once again.**"

**Friday, April 3, 1998:**

After Communion, I could see myself taken into a small tunnel area where I was withdrawn from the world, but I could still look back. Jesus said: "**My people, during Lent you should take notice of what is going on in your lives. When you stand back and look at the big picture of your life, you see sometimes how fruitless some of your wants and desires are. Your life here is very short, yet you have a lot to accomplish. Many times you see that** seeking the things of this world leaves you empty. Once you obtain one goal of wealth, you only seek more. But when you direct your life to serving Me and your neighbor, you have a greater joy in your heart. Money and things will never give you true happiness, because you are a spiritual being and your soul seeks its rest with Me. Until you realize love of Me and your neighbor are the most important in your life, your soul will be groping through life feeling empty. It is the graces of My love in the sacraments that reveal this sharing of love that ais so important. On your own you cannot come to know Me, but when you give your life over to My service, life will take on more meaning. Once you stop letting the desires of the world blind you, you will see more clearly what your real duties are on this earth. It is this understanding of the value of each soul that will drive you to see saving souls for Me is your most important duty. So let go of your own desires and seek to do My will."

Later, at Adoration, I could look down on a palatial estate with many guards around. Jesus said: "**My people, when you look on your political leaders, you are seeing men and women challenged by their greed for power. Power corrupts completely. Those, that make it to the top, have had to make many compromises. Drinking the wine of power and fame causes many to continue as far and as long as they can. The striving for more power is like those sick with a desire for more money. There is no end to which they will stop in their desire for more power as well. These leaders are so steeped in the worldly things that their morals have been corrupted for their gains. Remember that you cannot take power or money beyond the grave. Everyone has to answer to me at judgment for their deeds. So do not seek riches, power, or fame. They will never help you to gain heaven. Instead, desire to be humble and poor in spirit, so you may be open to follow My Will. When you follow My ways instead of the world's ways, you will be led to a heavenly kingdom beyond the riches of this life."**

**Saturday, April 4, 1998:**
After Communion, I could see a folding chair with a jacket hanging over it along with a trade profession hat. Jesus said: "**My people,**

you are only on this earth for a short time. Your coat on the chair indicates how quickly your time at work goes by. You are born, and your parents bring you up through high school. It seems only yesterday and you are now out of the house. Your life at work seems long, while you are working, but soon you are retired. You enjoy life for a time and then you are facing your death bed. For those, who live an average life, you are at Heaven's Gate before you know it. Some, who are taken earlier, go even quicker. My point is that you have little time to learn of the important things of life. You have to reach out and grab each moment possible to spend some time with your Lord. You are all called to do My work, but many want to do their own things instead. This Lenten time gives you an opportunity to slow down and make an accounting of where you are in life. Even this time is slipping away, since Holy Week is already approaching. If you are not spending enough time in prayer, you need to analyze your time more to fit it in. A spiritual man needs meditation time to make corrections in his behavior. You need to curb any of your vices, which are taking too much of your time from Me. I give you twenty-four hours, seven days a week. You should be able to find some time for Me each day. Someone, you love, needs to be told of your love every day. By the time you give Me each day, I will truly know how much you love Me."

Later, at Adoration, I could see a large letter 'Z' with a circle around it. Jesus said: "My people, I am the Alpha and the Omega. I am the Beginning and the End from A to Z. In the Scriptures I caused unrest in My people when I claimed that before Abraham came to be, I Am. When I made statements of My Divinity witnessed by My Father, they said that I was a blasphemer. But in essence, I was telling the very truth of why I came down upon the earth. I came to free you of your sins as the promised Redeemer, since Adam's sin. I am truly the King of the Universe. All creation has been brought into being through Me. Everything, that you see on earth, is there because of My Will. Be thankful and give Me praise and glory for all I have done for you. When you see how My power is almighty even over all the demons, you will understand how victory can only be Mine over sin, death, and evil. Following Me is like following the light of the sun. All angels and creatures give praise to their Creator. Even Satan bows before My power. So have no fear of him or his subjects. I am the victor, so come to me, My children, and I will protect you."

**Sunday, April 5, 1998:** (Palm-Passion Sunday)
After Communion, I could see a choir dressed in altar clothes and then Jesus came forward with a loving smile in a white tunic. Jesus said: **"My people, there is an irony in this week's celebration. For you are sharing in My victory over sin through My death on the Cross. At the beginning, the people of My day were joyful and triumphant on My riding into Jerusalem. Yet, they were the same crowds later who wanted to crucify Me. They were the same ones listening to Pilate and the high priests who wanted to kill Me for telling the truth of My Divinity. These leaders could not understand the reason for My Coming and yet they did not want the people to follow Me instead of them. I am the Lamb of God who was offered up for your redemption. It was only after the inspiration of the Holy Spirit and My own explanations later, that even My Apostles were made to understand how biblical prophecy had to be fulfilled. I love all of My creatures so much that I would die for them, even if only one had sinned against Me. My sacrifice was for all of mankind, those who died, those living, and those yet to come. This is why you should remember that I am still suffering for the sins being committed now. When you realize how I suffer in atonement for your sins at this time, you should try to minimize My pain by minimizing your sins. If you truly love Me, you would lead better lives and instruct those around you to come back to Me as well."**

Later, at Adoration, I could see a monstrance with a miracle of the Eucharist. Blood was coming on the Host. Jesus said: **"My people, there are many occurrences when My Hosts have bled or the wine has turned into blood. Many of these miracles of My Eucharist are to encourage your faith. But even more importantly, they witness the truth to My Transubstantiation of My Hosts into My Real Body and Blood. My Real Presence in the Hosts are witnessed when you see My Blood come forth.**

Many of the miracles have been proven to be Real Blood by the scientists. Even in the face of reality and technical proof, there are still many who do not believe in My Real Presence. This denial of My Presence is the worst of insults and a disrespect for My Gift of the Eucharist. This is why those same people, who reject My Presence, do not feel it necessary to confess their sins. Those, who teach against My Real Presence, and put down these miracles, are the real blasphemers. These are the ones that are removing the sacred and will be the ones drawn to the Antipope. Those, who do not love My Blessed Sacrament, are the lukewarm that I vomit from My mouth. They are like the Pharisees who give Me lip service, but their hearts are far from Me. If you do not have love for Me in your heart, how long can your faith last?"

Monday, April 6, 1998:

After Communion, I could see Padre Pio raising his hand and he said: "My children, this is the week that I suffered the most from the stigmata. For all the saints and those living with the stigmata, they are very familiar with the pain of this week. Even if you do not suffer this pain of Jesus, try to remember this week how much He had to suffer for you. There are many suffering servants also that are going through daily pain in reparation for the sins of man. If you have pain at any time, offer it up for your sins or the sins of others. Do not waste your pain or complain about it, but use it for a good purpose. Many are suffering injustices from various abusers. Pray for them that their problems may be resolved. When you think of me, build up your prayer life and continue a humble life."

Later, at Adoration, I could see a large number of bills of money wrapped together. Jesus said: "My people, you are going through Holy Week and re-enacting My betrayal for money by Judas. Today, many are betraying Me again in their lust for money, and all it may bring them in riches. Greed for money has become another god which man has raised up before Me as the golden calf of long ago. My people, come to your senses before it is too late. You are so caught up in your stock market, that you fail to see it has become another golden calf. Seek to live a

humble, quiet life in following My Will, instead of following
the desires to be rich in this life's goods. You cannot have two
masters, you will love one and hate the other. Seek the eternal
riches of heaven and refuse to be misled searching for this
world's treasure that will be gone tomorrow. I have given this
message many times. No matter how obvious this message is,
still some are more concerned with the world than the destination of their souls. Understand more where you are going after
this life, and that knowledge will set you back on a path to Me
in Heaven. Do not sell out your souls to the gods of this world."

**Tuesday, April 7, 1998:**

After Communion, I could first see the face of the Statue of Liberty and then the head band of stars turned to Our Lord's crown of thorns. Jesus said: **"My people of America, for years this statue has been a symbol of your being free and your rights of freedom. Your country was founded with Me at the center in your Declaration of Independence. But now you have abused your privileges and your country lies in moral decadence, where even My Commandments and prayer have been removed from your public buildings. You have so confused your freedoms and rights between church and state, that you are now a country embracing atheism to true religion. That is why you are seeing a crown of thorns, for as I suffered, many of My faithful will suffer persecution. Because of your actions in killing the unborn, and defying My laws through your sins of the flesh, your country will be plunged into ruin, where all of your freedoms will be stripped from you. Your hands will be held fast by another, and you will be a prisoner of a new tyrant, that will rule over the earth in the form of the Antichrist. Pray for My protection, as you will need My help to save your souls."**

Later, at the prayer group, I could see Jesus on the cross with many people looking upon Him. A large crowd spread out as far as you could see and a darkness came over the land. Jesus said: **"My people, the time of My Enlightenment is coming soon when all of mankind will look on Me and see the pain of their sins that I suffer. There will come a brief darkness over the land when all souls will be laid bare before Me. You will see how your lives would be judged before Me, but you will be given a short time to change your lives. This is your chance to seek the forgiveness of your sins in Confession. When this time comes, do not reject this last chance to repent for the many."**

I could see some very simple roofs in some small homes that will provide room for your underground Masses. Jesus said: **"My people, I have been asking you to prepare a place where My faithful can meet for Masses. The time of the coming schism grows near and you will be shut out of your churches. Your religious persecution will increase until you will have to go into hiding from the authorities. You have My assurance that I will not leave you. My Real Presence will be miraculously with you."**

I could see some sidewalks and people picketing a hospital to stop abortions. Jesus said: "**My people, do not forget the little innocent ones who are being murdered and crucified with Me. This is a dark hour over your country for all the abortions that you are committing. Go forward and make your voice heard against this genocide of your infants. You cried over the Holocaust of the Jews, but you have a greater holocaust going on every day in your hospitals. Show Me that you are concerned about this injustice by your very actions and prayers.**"

I could see a white pavement and a torrent of blood spilled on the ground. Jesus said: "**My people, the blood of your infants is being poured out before you in witness of the carnage of your abortions. You have seen some statues bleeding blood and also some people with the stigmata bleeding at this time. They are all bleeding to witness the effects of your sins of abortion against Me. Do everything in your power to discourage these mothers from killing their babies.**"

I could see the signs of spring coming in the green bushes and new flowers. Jesus said: "**My people, as you see the signs of new life coming in nature, lift up your hearts to share in the remembrance of My Resurrection. When I arose from the dead, I have given all of you a new hope when you will rise from the dead as well. Every time that you are forgiven your sins in Confession, you are like a new creation as My grace enlightens your drooping spirit. Strive to be cleansed of your sins and remain holy before Me by frequent Confession.**"

I could see Mary with her head down sorrowing before her Son's death. Mary said: "**My dear children, I suffered much as my heart was pierced by a sword to see my Son die at the hands of His own people. They failed to believe in His Words and His Divinity. But I knew this had to happen for all of mankind to be free to come to Heaven. This was a bitter sweet event that I had to suffer, but I glory in my Son's Redemption of man. His death on the Cross was the ultimate sacrifice to atone for all of the sins of mankind. Rejoice in my Son's victory over death and sin.**"

**Wednesday, April 8, 1998:**

After Communion, I could see a tomb opening in a hill. Jesus said: "**My people, I am burying your sins with Me, when I died** for you. This is how I treat all of your sins, when you seek My forgiveness. As you walk in the valley of death, you are strengthened by My sacrifice to continue through life in faith. Once you come to Me in judgment, you are buried with Me for a while. Then on that day of your glory, you will be resurrected with Me in Heaven. Because of Adam's sin, all of you are under the shroud of sin and death. But because of My rising again, you

can be raised again as well, if you follow My Will. So do not be afraid of death, but see it as a transition to the life in the spirit that will last forever. Know that your souls are immortal and they will pass by the grave. That is why living a faith filled life is necessary to be brought to Heaven with Me."

Later, after Communion, I could see a cross with flowers in a bouquet at the center. Then I saw flames coming from the cross but it was not being consumed. Jesus said: **"My people, look on My Cross as a symbol of life, for without Me, you have no life in you. That is the significance of the flowers that I am showing you, as life on the Cross through My death. The unquenchable fire symbolizes how much I love each of you, that I died for all of mankind. My burning love reaches out to every soul to welcome you to heaven. If you open your heart to Me, I can give you a burning desire to love Me and follow Me. I warm the coldest of hearts that are at least open to give Me a chance to reveal Myself to you. Those, who close their hearts to Me, I cannot force Myself on you. If you are to be saved, you must come to Me of your own free will. Pray for those sinners to have a proper disposition and may they be more open to invite Me into their hearts. Those, who accept Me, will have a treasure house of My love, and they will never regret giving their will over to Me."**

**Thursday, April 9, 1998:** (Holy Thursday)

After Communion, I could see some angels coming out from dark space. Then I saw a vision of thousands of angels descending slowly upon the earth. Along with them was an eerie red cloud that came slowly down over the earth and spread out in all directions. Jesus said: **"My people, you are seeing the wrath of God which will come down and torture all those who are unfaithful. My faithful will be protected in safe places, but the evil ones will receive a hell on earth. You are seeing how the many plagues will be brought down on those who rejected Me and tried My lambs. They will pay in physical sufferings for all of their sins for a time. Then these evil ones will be cast into hell. My faithful, I will then raise up and they will enjoy My renewed earth in an Era of Peace with no evil. Many of My loving souls have lived to see My day and their joy will be granted to them."**

**Friday, April 10, 1998:** (Good Friday)

After Communion, I could see a bare cross that was meant for each of us to carry. Jesus said: **"My people, you have witnessed to My dying on the Cross as a historical event. I died for you on this day, so that every soul would have an opportunity to come to Me. Each soul is given a particular cross that is a perfect fit for their capabilities and their strengths. If you were given a choice to pick anyone's cross, you would discover your own cross was the most comfortable. You all must face Me in judgment one day, and I will ask you if you lived up to carrying your own cross. Those, who took their cross and carried it to Heaven, have followed My Will and they will have their glorious resurrection in My Kingdom. Those, who refused to carry their crosses, will pay dearly in the life hereafter. I have asked each of you to accept your cross, because My yoke is easy and My burden is light."**

**Saturday, April 11, 1998:** (Easter Vigil)

After Communion, I could see a bright light in the sky that was radiating out from Jesus on His Resurrection. Jesus said: **"My dear faithful, at the time of My Resurrection there was a charge of radiant energy as evidenced by the Holy Shroud. Nothing could restrain or contain Me. I have created everything and it was only the God-Man being that I allowed any condescension of My appearance. When I became radiant and dazzlingly white, that is My natural form and why man cannot bear My presence unless I allow it. Many, who saw Me, did not recognize Me since I looked so different in My coloring. It was only with a gift of the Holy Spirit that I allowed My disciples to recognize Me. I am amazed that anyone could think that I could not control Satan. See that My power has crushed sin and death. Satan only has his will if I permit it. The time for his imprisonment in Hell is coming shortly. Trust wholly in My power and I will protect your souls. You will see Me coming on the clouds in all of My glory to declare My victory over evil and sin. This same radiance of My power at My Resurrection, you will see demonstrated again in the clouds to know that I am truly coming again."**

**Sunday, April 12, 1998:** (Easter Sunday)

After Communion, I could see Jesus standing there in a Church. Then I saw Mary and the Holy Spirit. Jesus said: **"My people, this is the day the Lord has made, rejoice that your salvation is here. The Gates of Heaven are now open again to those who follow Me. This is a joyous feast that all may celebrate My rising from the dead. Now you will realize the power I have over everything. Even in your day, where evil is rampant, rejoice because My victory will reign soon, again. You are seeing My mother and the Holy Spirit because they will play a role in My Second Coming. My mother will crush the head of Satan and the Holy Spirit will protect My people in the desert of the tribulation. Have no fear and this same Easter rejoicing will be yours once again when I come. Prepare yourselves and call down My angels to defend you."**

At Adoration, I could look out of the windows and see men coming to take people away to detention centers. Jesus said: **"My people, you will see the persecution come swiftly, as many are already in position to bring about a takeover in your country. Emphasis will be made on ridding all of the guns in your country. Already your soldiers are having their bases closed, or they will be moved overseas for indefinite amounts of time. You will be stripped of your military and police protection and a police state of United Nations foreign troops will be forced on you. By manipulation of your armies and control of your government by the One World people, you will be made outlaws with no freedoms. This will happen overnight, and no one will want to believe that it can happen. You will be like My people in the desert of the Exodus, seeking your freedom. This will be a time of tribulation when I will provide food, shelter, and water for all of those who have faith in Me. Follow Me at all times, because the unfaithful will have to suffer many times what you will be tested with. Warn the people to prepare their souls by seeking My forgiveness of their sins. Those, who refuse Me, will wish they had never been born, because their pain will be so great."**

**Monday, April 13, 1998:**

After Communion, I could see the curvature of the earth and a bright burst of light shone from down on the earth. Jesus said: **"My** people, many times you do not realize the scope of My power in My Resurrection. I died on the Cross for all of the people on the earth for all time. That means for all of those souls that lived before Me, those living in My time, and for all those souls who are to live after Me. This includes souls yet to be born, as well as all those living today. The grace of My forgiveness is offered to everyone, such that you should no longer fear the evil one. This planet has been graced that I came in historic time to especially redeem you for your sins. This speck out of all of the universe has seen My saving power. Put everything you see in perspective as My Creation and you can understand how awesome is My power and My love for each of you. Give praise and thanksgiving to Me for all of the many gifts that I have bestowed on each of you. Rejoice, that My loving protection from evil reaches out to help you, if you would only follow My Will."

Later, at Adoration, I could see some massive winds and tornadoes blowing everything apart. Jesus said: **"My people, a time is coming when you will be stripped of all of those possessions that you had trusted in for your survival. Your homes will be at risk from many natural disasters. Your wealth will be stolen from you by the One World people. You will see storms with a severity never seen before, because these will be enhanced by the weather machines. You will see your money manipulated away from you in stock market control. You are controlled by the One World people in almost every aspect of your life even down to your medicines. If you depend only on your own achievements or your wealth, you will be confounded. If you rely on faith in Me and My protection, I will lead you safely to Heaven. You cannot succeed without My help. So do not depend on your money, which will be taken from you either legally or illegally. Depend solely on Me and you will win the battle for your soul and others."**

### Tuesday, April 14, 1998:

After Communion, I could see through a skylight at some branches. Jesus said: **"My people, I am the vine and you are the branches. He, who lives in Me, shares with the Father as well. Because of My Eucharistic offering, I gave My church a new** foundation in My Real Presence. I have given you all new life by being a part of My Mystical Body. That is why if two or more of you are present, I am there in your midst. Not only are you a part of Me, but apart from Me you are nothing. So hold fast to Me in frequent Confession, and My Grace will always keep you close to My Heart."

Later, at Adoration, I could see a lot of cells multiplying as some kind of disease was spreading. Jesus said: "My people, I am showing you one of the diseases of your pestilence that will cause some deaths. There will come upon you an airborn disease of suspicious origin. It will have the symptoms of a severe case of pneumonia, only the doctors will have difficulty in developing a cure. This will come from a planned germ warfare to cut down on the population. As the time of the tribulation comes, you will find a healing for many of the coming plagues at My places of refuge. Many also will have healing powers to cure My faithful. Have no fear of these things, nor the power of the Antichrist, for I will be victorious over everything. Have patience for a time, and I will deliver My remnant from the hands of the evil ones."

**Wednesday, April 15, 1998:**

After Communion, I could see a large Church and only a small number attending Mass. Jesus said: "My people, when I return, will I find any of My faithful waiting for Me? If you are weak now in following My Commandments with little restrictions, how are you to follow Me when the time of the religious persecution comes? There is a faithful remnant, who will stick by Me no matter what comes. Many others come to Me because it is convenient or a social gesture. Your faith's real meaning will be tested shortly. There will come a time when your life may be at stake for your beliefs in Me. Remember that this life is nothing and that you are struggling to keep My Word, so you can share with Me in Heaven in the next life. Be prepared to choose Me only over all the world has to offer. When the Antichrist comes, you will be forced to choose Me when it will take more courage to stand up for what you believe. Do not be afraid to declare your allegiance to Me publicly."

**Thursday, April 16, 1998:**

After Communion, I could see Churches, but they all had blank concrete structures on the front. Jesus said: **"My people, the coming schism in My Church will be your first assault on the church structures. The Antipope will take control of all of the Catholic churches, and My remnant will have their Masses underground in their homes for a while. Once the Antichrist comes to power, only a few of these churches will be protected. Most of the church buildings will be either destroyed or made into museums. A religious persecution will come over your land that will threaten all of the lives of My faithful with martyrdom. You will see a holocaust against My believers as the Jews were abused and killed. This age of evil will grow worse for a time. Then just as the Antichrist gains control over the world, I will come and smite him and throw him into Hell. You must be strong in faith during this tribulation, and trust wholly in My help and protection. Without seeking My help, you would be completely lost. Your Savior awaits every soul willing to do My Will. Do not be misled by the world, but stay close to My side for help."**

Later, at the prayer group, I could see needles for shots being given on the right and on the left. Jesus said: **"My people, beware of those doctors that are manipulating vaccines being given out, especially to your military. Under innocent reasons to protect people from diseases, these means can be abused by those seeking to control your populations. Lethal viruses can be planted in the people in this way."**

I could see a bright ray of light shining forth from the heart of Jesus as in the Divine Mercy. Jesus said: **"My people, My Divine love is shining My graces and mercy upon you as you draw closer to Mercy Sunday. I am always available to you in granting you forgiveness of your sins. You have been blessed with My Sacraments of Reconciliation and My Eucharist. See that you be purified of your sins in Confession before you receive Me in Holy Communion."**

I could see a hand print in blood as it covered the Capital Building. Jesus said: **"My people, how blind are your lawmakers when they authorize killing infants and older people? When a mandate of the people does not rise up against these injustices, all** of your country must take the blame for these evil laws. Work and pray that these laws against My Commandments may be struck down. If these laws are not changed, your chastisements in destruction will continue to increase in intensity."

I could see many speakers in the shape of megaphones. Jesus said: "My people, you have witnessed the celebration of My Easter Resurrection. This is the good news for all of mankind that needs to be shouted from the rooftops. I rose from the dead in a glorified body to witness to you My power over sin and death. Rejoice that I am calling you to follow Me into the next life. Those, who give Me homage and give thanks for My gifts, will merit the gift of eternal life. Those, who do not choose to follow Me, will be swallowed up by the desires of the world and will be the deadest of the dead."

I could see some women coming to the tomb. Jesus said: "My people, the readings this week point to the beauty and the difference of My glorified body. You also will receive a glorified body, if you follow My Will. The realization of My rising after three days in the tomb was finally understood as I visited the Apostles and ate fish with them. Blessed are those who believe in Me and yet have never seen Me."

I could see a handle as to a suitcase for traveling. Jesus said: "My son, continue to spread My Good News of My Resurrection and prepare the people for My Second Coming. Be steadfast in your desire to bring souls back to Me out of love or out of the fear of punishment in Hell. Many are going through life with no care to where their soul is headed. The more souls you can make aware of Me in the short time left, the more souls you can bring to Me before it is too late."

I could see some people dressed in white and in the next scene they were all laying on the ground asleep. Jesus said: "My people, beware of the signs that the false witnesses will perform to try and lead you astray. The evil ones, who will persecute you, will show great signs in the sky and miracles before you. Do not believe in anyone else but Me. I am the lamp of light to show you the way. I will be seen coming on the clouds of Heaven to judge this age. Do not follow any others claiming to be Me. Do not take any sign or Mark of the Beast for buying and selling.

Be willing to give up your life before accepting anything from the Antichrist. No matter whether they claim you need these Marks for food or jobs, refuse to be controlled by the evil one. Trust in Me and I will provide for all of your needs."

**Friday, April 17, 1998:**
After Communion, I could see an altar and there were two pulpits next to each other. In the one pulpit a nun was giving the homily. Jesus said: "**My people, I am again showing you this coming split in My Church indicated by the two pulpits. You will be forced to choose between the church of the Antipope or the church of My remnant which is led by Pope John Paul II. Those, who follow the Antipope, will be defying the laws and traditions set up by My Apostles. When you see this group claiming to be the true church and defying My laws, then you will have proof of this apostasy in My church. I will still be with you in My remnant, but do not follow those teachings against My Commandments. Eventually, this evil pope will be misleading the people to follow the Antichrist. This blasphemy will be the desolation of abomination that will control the chair of St. Peter. I have given you many messages concerning this schism in My Church, because it will be very subtle and will confuse many. See when Pope John Paul II leaves Rome or is claimed dead, that the schism will begin. This is the warning to go into hiding, since the Antichrist will soon take power and imprison and kill all of those against the New World Order."**

Later, at Adoration, I could look into a stream of water and see a reflection of the sky. Jesus said: "**My people, when you look closely at My Creation, you see a reflection of My love. Everything that has been made, was very good, because the idea of its being came from the mind of God. I have willed everything into being from the start by My Own fixed Will of its existence. Even the duration of your own existence is a continuation of My desire to let it be. Life of itself is a gift to be treasured and not to be destroyed. It is only the desire of the evil one that death should be spread among you. The evil one has a hate of your life and he despises all of My Creation, especially man. This is why he wishes to cause each of you to sin against Me, so he can claim victory** over your soul. Yet, I have defeated Satan by dying as a man for the salvation of your souls. My loving arms reach out to each soul to bring you to Me in Heaven. Give in to the desire of your soul to follow My Will. When you love Me and are in complete harmony with My Commands, you will be brought to the goal of your soul's eternal rest with me forever."

**Saturday, April 18, 1998:**

At St. Joseph's Church, Thibodaux, Louisiana, after Communion, I could see Jesus standing in a bright white tunic. Jesus said: **"My people, as I appeared to some of the women and My disciples, the others found it hard to believe that I had truly risen from the dead in a glorified body. For some, I had to give physical signs that I was alive and present and not just a ghost. St. Thomas felt My wounds and believed, but blessed are they who have not seen and have believed. My friends, even today you have doubting Thomases in My Real Presence in My Eucharistic Host. You, My son, have witnessed many miracles of My Hosts bleeding. These miracles were shown for all to prove to you that I am really present body and blood in the Consecrated Bread and Wine. So believe in My Real Presence and believe that I resurrected to show you that I have conquered sin and death. I gift all of My sacraments and My life to you out of love, so you can have your souls saved by the ransom of My Blood. Follow Me as I asked My Apostles and do My Will. Those, who believe and obey My commands, will rejoice one day with Me in Heaven."**

**Sunday, April 19, 1998:** (Mercy Sunday)

At Christ the Redeemer Church Adoration, Thibodaux, Louisiana, I could see Jesus standing in front of me and He brought me close to see His wounds in His hands. Jesus said: **"My people, when you come before Me in Holy Communion or in Adoration of My Blessed Sacrament, look on me as pure love. My mercy is poured out on you. My love is poured out on you. My graces are poured out on you. Come as St. Thomas and place your hand in My wounds, so you are united in My wounds of love. Become fully immersed in My sufferings that I offered up** for all of your sins. It is when you understand how much I suffered for each of your souls, that you can taste a little of how much I love you. When you are wrapped in My arms of love, I will be protecting you from all of the Devil's temptations. When you walk in My Divine Will, you are assured of your salvation with Me. See, My children, that you bring all souls with you, and take their hands and place them in My wounds as well, so that they can be made believers. It is this missionary spirit that should draw all of My faithful to witness to all men of My love and My mercy. Bring the lost souls to Me, so I can bathe them in My graces of love, and I can protect them from evil as yourselves. When I wash your souls of your sins in the forgiveness of Confession, I make all of you into a new creation, where grace abounds in your souls. Come, My children, do not delay, but go out to all nations and evangelize in My Name. Bless those souls in My most Precious Blood, so all souls will be open to My saving power."

Later, at Christ the Redeemer Church, Thibodaux, Louisiana, after Communion, I could see the Host and the chalice full of wine. Jesus said: "**My people, as you come to receive Me in Holy Communion and the wine, you are sharing again in My Last Supper when I broke bread with My Apostles. This is the living bread that I share with you that a man may never die. When you take My Eucharist into your bodies, you become little tabernacles of My Presence. This is why each soul is so precious to Me, because you are all temples of the Holy Spirit. Remember this when you meet anyone in the street, that each soul has Me present. So when you see someone in need and you help them, you are helping Me as well. At the same time, I will hold you responsible for when you fail to help someone, because you failed to help Me. So when you see another person, look and see My Presence in everyone as well. This is why I have always asked you to love God and your neighbor as yourself.**"

**Monday, April 20, 1998:**

After Communion, I could see some guns on an altar in a Church. Jesus said: "**My people, I have told you and St. Peter that those, who live by the sword, will die by the sword. When** the tribulation comes, you are not to take up arms, because you will be fighting principalities and powers. Prayer and your sacramentals will be your weapons, as your angels and I will fight your battles for you. The guns on the altar will be how evil men will keep you from entering the churches. My faithful will be tested with a religious persecution where you will have to share your faith in secret. Just as I told My Apostles, they will bind your hands against your will and carry you off to prison. Evil men will hate you and despise you for teaching in My Name. But if you truly believe in Me, you will never deny Me and you will stand up for your beliefs, even if it requires your life from you. Do not be afraid at that time, for I will give you what to say and what to do. Even if you are martyred for My Name, I will grant you your eternal reward with Me in Heaven."

Later, at Adoration, I could see some colored lights in the sky and they had various shapes and sizes. Jesus said: "**My people, no matter what signs the Antichrist will display for you, remember that he is not Me and can never be Me. All those, who are evil, are cold and ruthless in their power. They do not know love, but he will be allowed to show miracles and illusions. Remember he will be inspired with lies, so do not believe him, even if he claims to be Me. I healed people of their sins and cured their ills out of love and compassion. You will recognize the Antichrist in his actions and in his fruits. You know a bad tree cannot give forth good fruit. When you see this tyrant, he will crave for power and blaspheme God. Be prepared for him by what I am showing you. Even if someone can show miraculous powers, you need to test the spirit for its source of power. Even Satan can appear in illusions as an angel of light. Pray to Me, My faithful, so you may be strengthened to endure this evil age and not be misled by these evil powers."**

### Tuesday, April 21, 1998:

After Communion, I could see a bell in front of me indicating freedom. Jesus said: "**My people, by My Redemption you are a new creation, an Easter People. You have been freed from the bondage of sin because of My victory over sin. The power of evil has been brought low and the Gates of Heaven are now** open once again. As those, who looked on the serpent on Moses' staph, were healed of their affliction, you too are now released from your sins. It is this ransom of your souls by My blood on the Cross that you are set free. Because you have been graced with this opportunity to enter into Heaven, come forward and receive My forgiveness of your sins in Confession. In order to take advantage of this open door to Heaven, you must accept My Will and follow the design for your life in My plan for you. When you make Me your personal Savior by accepting My Commands, you will have the promise of your salvation granted to you. Those, who have faith in Me, I will see to your protection and you will abide with Me in Heaven."

Later, at Adoration, I could look down a long rich garden from an estate. Jesus said: **"My people, many of the super rich people have gone beyond the desire for money. These one world people have their designs on controlling the world through their power. Their organizations are even diabolical in their plans as they promote the death culture of Satan. Satan hates man, and He has tempted certain organizations to promote abortions, wars and killing in any way possible for profit. These men are plotting to reduce the population so they can have more control. They are preparing the way for the Antichrist in his religious persecution. Many groups as the Christians, those fighting abortions, and those seeking to preserve proper morals in the family, are being targeted for persecution. These trials are subtle, but devious in their means to promote Satan's plans. Pray much, My faithful, for you will be dearly tested for your faith in Me. Never fear, but trust in My protection as I will be the victor in the end. Never lose hope even when the odds against you are many."**

### Wednesday, April 22, 1998:

After Communion, I could see inside a whale with its organs and skeleton structure. Jesus said: **"My son, I am leading you like Jonah, so you can warn the people. You may wonder if all that you are doing is having an effect on the people. I assure you that bringing even a few souls to Me would be worth your effort. But in fact many are being touched by My Words to** their souls. Do not falter in your resolve and continue your constant prayers for souls. You have understood rightly that saving souls is your most important task on earth. Evangelizing My world is important, especially as the End Times of the Antichrist are about to descend on you. Prepare the people by having them seek My forgiveness of their sins. Seek My help and you will be saved."

**Thursday, April 23, 1998:**
After Communion, I could see a large pyramid and some snow at the top indicating very high degree Masons. Jesus said: "**My people, the Masonic Order is led at the top by very powerful and influential men. They run companies or world organizations that affect the lives of all men and women. These are not only rich people seeking after money, but they also are seeking worldly power. In addition, this group is very much into worshiping Satan and follows the will of Satan, instead of Me. They understand astrology and follow the rituals of the occult with special attention to certain numerology. These are the ones setting up the United Nations to control the world. Through international financiers they control the money and the heads of state. These will be the ones to cause your religious persecution. They will be the ones also preparing the way for control by the Antichrist. They are the One World people setting up the smart cards and the Mark of the Beast in preparation for the New World Order. They will be setting up secret lists to do away with all those that stand in their way to rule over men. Pray, My children, for the souls of these people, for their hearts are cold and hideous. Have no fear of them, for My faithful I will protect from the Devil's clutches. I will be victorious over all of their plans and they, who continue to follow Satan, will taste the wrath of My justice.**"

Later, at the prayer group, I could see an altar and people were worshiping a wooden face of a god. Jesus said: "**My people, you have many idols that you worship in this evil age. Your TVs, sporting events, financial investments and the like have become little gods for you. These things occupy your time and attention more than the time that you give Me. These are worldly things** that are cold and could never love you. Give Me your worship only and refuse to let these idols control you."

I could see a large image of a man placed over a body for a tombstone. Jesus said: "My people, many take pride in leaving their mark on the world when they die. My children, do not take pride in yourself or seek to be famous in this life. When you die, none of your fame will go with you to the judgment. In time people will soon forget you. Seek to store heavenly treasures in what you do. Being prayerful and humble will raise you higher in heaven than lauding your accomplishments."

I could see a classy showroom for cars. Jesus said: "My people, many do things deliberately for show to impress their friends. I assure you when you do deeds for show on earth, you already have been repaid. When you do good works or donate to the poor, do these things in secret and My heavenly Father will repay you. When you do things on earth, seek to do them for others and not just for yourself."

I could see a full moon in the night and then Mary appeared with the moon under her feet. Mary said: "My dear children, I am the lesser light compared to the brightness of the sun in my Jesus. I am the reflection of His light as all of us are made to His image. If you are to be my Son, Jesus' disciple, you must give witness of His Word to others. I have come to prepare you for His Second Coming. Rejoice in His resurrection as you await His Coming again."

I could see some large trucks strip mining and abusing the land. Jesus said: "My people, you do lip service to try and protect your environment on earth. But you are in too much love of your lifestyle to really make meaningful changes. For your comfort you consume the resources of the earth beyond what can be replenished. Your influence on your weather is just one aspect of the effects of your abuse on nature. These things you are doing will take their revenge on your comforts."

I could see a mother in the home caring for her children. Jesus said: "My people, why is your society so consumed with having a rich material life? By turning your efforts toward many paychecks for the good life, you have compromised proper care for your children. Many have wondered why their children are doing the immoral things they do. A better home life and a better environment would show your true love and care for your children's attention. The extra money is never worth your personal working with your children. Your society breeds its troubles by the way it abuses its children in day care and TV babysitters."

I could see a beautiful sunset with red and yellow colors. Jesus said: "My people, as you look toward the sunset of your life, seek to understand the real meaning of My Resurrection. I am truly eternal life for you, and those who follow Me, will receive a just reward. Do not wait until your final days to start preparing for your death. Every day should be lived as your last, because you know not how long you will live. So start today with a new plan to prepare for the next life in all that you do. When you consecrate your lives to Me in following My Will, all that you do will be stored up in Heaven for you. This is the living death to self and a new life in the spirit that you are called to. See the real beauty of My Resurrection by living one day for your own resurrection with Me."

**Friday, April 24, 1998:**

After Communion, I could see a large crack in a pew in a Church. Jesus said: "My people, every one of you have your own imperfections as sinners. Your own weaknesses are a way of keeping you humble, so you do not get puffed up with pride. Do not despair in your faults, but always be working to compensate for them. By your good works and prayers, you can carry forward with a good Christian life. Remember to give good example to others in your actions, so you are not hypocrites. Build up each other's faith and unite My faithful in any cases of division. By your joyful outlook, you can encourage people around you. Do not be looking only to complain or gossip about other people's imperfections. When you show love to everyone, it helps to bring peace to those to whom you are witnessing."

**Saturday, April 25, 1998:** (St. Mark)

At St. Cecilia's, Rockaway, New Jersey, after Communion, I could see a modern large opal shape and then an older nun was seen. Jesus said: "My people, some of your priests and nuns have lost their vocations to the allurements of the world. Even your environment for new vocations has discouraged many who have come forward to seek the priesthood. Your evil age has turned many to think more of themselves than to please Me. It takes devotion to Me and a sense of giving to others for a vocation to mature. Pray for vocations both to the priesthood and the sisterhood. Pray also for those that answer My Call, that they may be encouraged to endure any hardships to continue in their priestly education. Those, who aspire to the priesthood, are very blessed in this age. So do everything to help them to answer My Call. The priests are very needed to share My Sacraments in a land where the laborers are so few. Continue to pray also for those other clergy to be faithful to their vocations."

At Sacred Heart Church, Rockaway, New Jersey, after Communion, I could see an angel in flight. I asked permission for my angel, Mark, to give a message. Mark said: **"I stand before God and give Him praise. See that when Jesus asked St. Peter three times if he loved Jesus, it was to remind Him of the three times St. Peter denied him. So it is every day for all the souls that deny Jesus in their sins. When you truly love someone, you need to affirm that love often. We angels are forever praising God and showing Him of our love in our service to Him. So it should be with all of God's creatures. Even though you all are in a weakened state, you have your guardian angels to call on for your help. We are examples of love for you to follow. Listen to the words of Jesus and truly live His message of love."**

### Sunday, April 26, 1998:

At the Mother Cabrini Chapel, Queens, New York, after Communion, I could see Mother Cabrini dressed in black and then I could see some leaves fallen as in the fall season. Mother Cabrini said: **"My son, thank you for coming to my chapel and for all of your devotions to me. This is where I did most of my work in receiving new immigrants. You, yourself, have been true to your call from Jesus in helping souls. Always be prayerful and remain humble in your work. When you seek to do His work, Jesus will provide for your needs. It is faith and trust in His** words that everyone is called to. Never falter in your resolve to evangelize souls for Jesus. Go now on your mission, as I and the Lord will help you."

Later, at St. Mary's Church, Queens, New York, after Communion, I could see some strong arches inside of a Church. Jesus said: "My people, I rejoice to be with My faithful at every Sacrifice of the Mass. My Real Presence comes among you in My Sacred Host. As you come to My Church, look to My strength I have given it, from the day I gave the keys to St. Peter in his profession of love for Me. Throughout the years I have upheld My Church through the work of My Apostles and their successors. Support and pray for My Pope son, John Paul II, who is leading My Church today. A day will come when My shepherd will be tested with your evil age. But even if he must be exiled, I will remain with you in My Spiritual Communion until the End Time."

**Monday, April 27, 1998:**

At St. Cecilia's Church, Rockaway, New Jersey, after Communion, I could see a house and outside of it on the ground I could see the Ark of the Covenant ready to be carried in haste. Jesus said: "My people, you are seeing My nomadic people in the Israelites. When they moved about, they carried My Presence about in the Ark of the Covenant. When it came to rest, they would store it in the Holy of Holies among the tents. So it will be in the time of the tribulation. The Antipope and his followers will control the churches. My remnant will have underground Masses when a priest is present. When a priest is not present, you will store and preserve My Presence in the Host. You will carry Me around from place to place, so you will always have My Real Presence among you. When Holy Communion is not available, you will call upon Me in Spiritual Communion, and My angels will deliver My Host to your tongues. Have faith and hope in Me, My children, for I will not leave you orphans."

Later, I could see an outdoor scene of a statue of the Infant of Prague. Then I saw a picture of a cross behind Him. Jesus said: "My people, I am asking you to focus on My Kingship over all of the people, even the unbelievers. As you witnessed during My passion, My betrayers mocked My Kingship. They did not even want to recognize My Divinity, even though they had witnessed My miracles. But I am presenting Myself as an infant king, because I am not a stern ruler, ready to punish you in an instant. No, I am a warm, merciful and loving king, who wants to raise up even the most unworthy of sinners. The innocence and joy of a baby is how I look at all of My creatures. You are all My subjects, because without Me, you would be nothing. But I give you free will to come and love Me by your own decision. I do not force My love on anyone, but I ask you as one, who loves you infinitely, to return your love to Me. Seek to do My Divine Will by carrying your cross through life and I will reward you by raising you up to Heaven with Me. Love Me with the simple love of a baby for My sake only, and do not worry about anything else that may try and interfere with loving Me."

**Tuesday, April 28, 1998:**

After Communion, I could see a lock and some handcuffs. Jesus said: **"My people, in today's reading about St. Stephen's stoning, this is an example of the ongoing suffering that My disciples must endure. Throughout biblical history, man has continually rejected the prophets that encouraged them to reform their lives. Man is too loving of his comforts of the flesh to willingly subdue them. It is this resistance to My laws that has caused the martyrdom and the harassment of My prophets. Those, who proclaim the Gospel and charge the people with obeying My laws, have been subjected to much ridicule and criticism. All of My prophets and messengers have had to endure this persecution through the years and it will get only worse in the tribulation. So go, My children, and speak out now while you have time, for soon your enemies will lay hold of you and your torture will begin. All those, who are faithful to My call, will reap their rewards in Heaven. So fear not what these evil men can do to the body, it is their effect on people's souls that is the most to be concerned about."**

Later, at Adoration, I could see a crucifix from the side and it was hanging on a wall in a house. Jesus said: **"My people, I am showing you how you need to have your sacramentals on your** walls at home. Have them blessed and place a crucifix, a statue, or an icon in every room of your house. In that way, no matter what room you are in, you will have a remembrance of Me and the saints. Even if you could have a holy water place at your entrance, it would help drive the evil spirits away. In all of your devotions, you witness to your love of Me by placing these little altars throughout your house. When you witness to Me before men, I will witness for you before My Father."

**Wednesday, April 29, 1998:**
After Communion, I could see a view going further and further back into a stone cave. Jesus said: "**My people, in the readings you are seeing how the early Christians were being persecuted. Eventually, they were hiding in the catacombs to avoid being captured. So it is in the vision, that during the tribulation, you will be provided with caves to hide where it is hilly, and places of holy ground where it is flat. I will be providing shelter and food for My elect, when they are put to the trial. Some will be martyred, while others will be led by their angels to safety. Have faith and hope that I will provide for all that you ask of me. I will not reject anyone who seeks to be saved, but everyone will have to suffer as I did. You will either suffer at the hands of your tormentors for Me, or those, who refuse Me, will suffer in hell on earth and below. This is not an easy life, but one of testing how sincerely you love Me. It is easy to love Me when it is convenient, but will you still love Me under duress?**"

**Thursday, April 30, 1998:**
After Communion, I could see a tree and as I moved around it, there were spotlights moving on it as well. Jesus said: "**My people, in the reading St. Phillip explains the Isaiah passage to the Ethiopian eunuch of My Coming as a lamb to be sacrificed. This is an example of a fulfilled prophecy when I died on the Cross for all of mankind's sins. In the vision you are seeing the tree of life as it was in the Garden of Eden. The tree of forbidden fruit, which Adam and Eve ate, resulted in the sin which cast them from the garden. This Tree of the Knowledge of Good and Evil became a tree of death as they were now condemned to die.**

Again, an old prophecy was given that I would come and redeem mankind for this sin of Adam. Now, you are seeing this prophecy fulfilled when you look on Me on the Cross as the new Tree of Life. By My dying on the Cross, this Tree of Death comes alive with My Resurrection. This sacrifice of My life was the atonement for Adam's sin. By this act of Mine, man now has new life as well, since you can now enter into Heaven. So when you read the Scriptures, look for the hidden meaning of the words in understanding how each prophecy must be fulfilled. As you approach the End Days, even the words of Revelation are being fulfilled in your hearing."

Later, at the prayer group, I could see a bush and behind the bush I saw Jesus come in radiant light in His glorified Body. God the Father said: "I AM presents My Son in all of His glory in a glorified body. You have treasured My Son's every word given to you by the Scriptures. Treasure also His Resurrection, for in this act of His glory you are all forgiven and given an example of your own resurrection. Have faith in following My Commandments and you, too, will be able to recognize your Savior."

I saw a large suspension bridge across the waters. Jesus said: "My people, I am the bridge between this world and the next world. You cannot come to the Father unless you come through Me. By My death and suffering, I have enabled you to cross into Heaven. All Heaven gives praise and glory to Me. When you reach your place in Heaven, you will rejoice to share in the Communion of Saints."

I could see a plain outdoor Indian dwelling. Jesus said: "My people, you have too many comforts and blessings for your own good. If you were to lead a simpler life, you would have more time for prayer and meditation. That is why when you are stripped of your possessions, you will see how little you can survive on with My help. Focus on serving Me in this world and put aside the excess cares of the world."

I could see some very modern looking shapes and furniture, yet many were still committing sins of fornication. Jesus said: "My people, no matter how much the evil one will glorify the pleasures of the flesh, do not violate My Commandment against adultery. He will tell you it is love and not a sin. Even some of

My clergy will not direct you properly. It is a mortal sin to fornicate, masturbate, or use birth control devices. Do not violate those acts to be cherished only under the bond of marriage. Many souls are lost to Hell because they listen to Satan's call to sins of the flesh. By prayer and Confession you can keep your souls clean. Even if you fail, pick up your cross and seek the forgiveness of your sins."

I could see small arrows of love to show signs of human romance. Jesus said: "My people, love between a man and woman is a normal drive placed in each of you. In this courting time it is important that both lead chaste lives before marriage. Living together without the marriage sacrament defies My laws and is nothing more than fornication. Without My blessing of the union, you are in constant danger of sin, so avoid this state of life. Just as fornication is a mortal sin, acts of homosexual unions are also mortal sins and this lifestyle should also be avoided. I have set My laws of life before you so life can come forth from the blessed union in My families. Those, who choose to violate My laws, will call down My wrath of justice upon them."

I could see a metal satellite coming right toward me in the sky. Jesus said: "My people, these satellites will control many means of your life in the New Age of the One World Order. Unless you use the chips and electronics of the world, you may not buy and sell. This control will be brought upon you in a very short time. You will have a choice to refuse this Mark of the Beast, but you will be an outlaw to defy the authorities. Do not be a part of this New Age Movement and do not take the chip in the hand even if they threaten you with death. Depend on My grace and help and your soul will survive the tribulation. You will be taunted by many desires of the world, but choose Me over anything that the world has to offer."

I could look on some newly dug grave sites. Jesus said: "My people, you are living in preparation for the one day that you should die. All of you are appointed to die from the day that you are born. There is a certain feeling of how final death can be. There is no turning back, no second chance. When your life is over, you will be judged forever on what you have done with your life. Your lifetime by any measure is short. That is why every moment should be valuable in seeking your salvation. **By loving Me and your neighbor, you will be directed to Heaven. In your short time seek to please Me in prayer and your good works. By seeking My forgiveness in Confession, you will always be in readiness to receive Me. So be on guard every day for that hour when I will call you home. It is the wise man who keeps his spiritual house in order that will join Me in Heaven. The lazy man in sin will one day be caught unawares and he will have to suffer in Hell for an eternity."**

**Friday, May 1, 1998:** (St. Joseph, the worker)
After Communion, I could see some nuns as the sisters of St. Joseph and then St. Joseph came and said: **"My dear children, give thanks for the work of the nuns in my Name for all they have done, especially teaching here. Pray much for their vocations and for those remaining to be dedicated to God in their work. Also, as my feast indicates, pray much for those laboring with their hands to feed and provide for their families. In an unsettled world, pray that your people will have sufficient jobs provided to afford a fair living. Pray also that the employers do not abuse their workers in giving them a just pay and proper working conditions."**

Later, at Adoration, I could see a prison with chains. Jesus said: **"My people, you have seen how St. Peter and St. John the Baptist had to suffer in prison with chains for their being faithful to Me. You in America have not had to suffer much in the way of persecution. It may even be difficult for some to imagine such a scourge of religious persecution coming to your land. Take courage, My children, even if you must suffer for My Name in your tribulation. As the evil one reaches the height of his power, you may have to endure being tortured. Call on My help and grace to never give in to this evil lot. No matter how much they will brain wash you with the occult or worship of the Antichrist, never lose faith in My love. These evil spirits will not have power over your souls, because of My power. They may torment you or even martyr you, but with Me at your side, I will protect your soul. So have no fear of these evil spirits and evil men, for I will overpower them and they will all be cast into Hell, where**

J. TEPELYA

they will then have to face their own chains. My power is almighty and they will not be able to prevent My victory. Without this testing, I would never know the depth of your love for Me. So fight the good battle against all evil that you will face."

**Saturday, May 2, 1998:**
At Christ the King Adoration, Atlanta, Ga. I could see Jesus in the Host of a monstrance. Then I saw another scene on TV showing a large circular coin of the new EURO held up as a monstrance. Jesus said: **"My people, I have given of myself, so you can have Me present in the Host. You have My Living Bread among you, which came from My Sacrifice of the Mass. My suffering and death are intimately connected to My Eucharist. The bread and wine are changed into My Body and Blood, so all of you may eat and share in the bread of Heaven. It is My Real Presence in the Host that you are adoring and giving praise. On the worldly side, you are seeing this new 'Euro' money praised for its innovation and stability of one currency for Europe. It is significant how they held this money up so it could be worshiped by the other worldly. The power of money has so possessed people, that they treat it as a god of itself. They even placed it on a pedestal so it could be seen by all as a symbol of monetary power. My people need to worship Me only as your loving and living God. Money and things of the world are cold and useless to the spirit. There is no love in things of the world. These are only distractions of the evil one to take you away from Me. These things are creations or the works of man. They are not God in themselves. I am love and the ultimate desire of your soul. Seek Me and you will have everlasting life. If you seek only the things of earth, you will be left in the deep nothingness of Hell."**

**Sunday, May 3, 1998:**
At Christ the King Church, after Communion, Atlanta, Ga., I could see a mother with her child. Jesus said: **"My people, I love you so much, as I am calling you, My children, in a spiritual way. Every soul I am calling to Myself, so they may know and appreciate My love for them. The little children have a special place in My heart. They are the innocent and open souls which**

I wish all of you could become. It is this spirit of a little child that I ask everyone to have in coming to Heaven. This is why it is so important for you to bring the children to Me so they can know and understand the sacredness of My Real Presence. The priest was praying for vocations, but without knowing of My love, how can My Call be known to anyone. So bring the children to Mass and My Adoration and they will be able to drink in My Heavenly graces. Teach them the faith taught by the Apostles, and let them embrace Me in My Sacraments. By laying this fertile ground for these young souls, they will be open if they wish to answer My Call to the religious life. Do not discourage such calls but embrace them with My love and show the children how beautiful it is to share your love with Me. If some receive a call to the religious life, build them up and never let a vocation go wanting. My laborers are few and many more are needed, especially in this evil age."

Later, at Adoration, I could look down on some furniture being moved around in a house. Jesus said: "My people, I am indicating to you that you will see some changes made in your lives. Some will do some moving out of choice, while others will be forced to move. Economic changes and job changes will precipitate these moves. I have told you that events will be changing at a fast pace. Those, seeking power through various organizations, will soon start to show their plans. As more things come under the control of a few, you will have to start making some serious choices in following the Antichrist or not. When you decide to put your full trust in Me and leave your homes and jobs behind, I will provide for you in all of your needs. Do not be fearful, but follow your heart in what I will call you to do."

**Monday, May 4, 1998:**

After Communion, I could see one color of fabric split in two down the middle. Jesus said: "My people, I have come to join all peoples into one loving family and to mend all the divisions caused by the evil one. It is the evil one's intention to get you quarreling among yourselves. He breeds hate, while I encourage love. That is why there is always this ongoing struggle between good and evil. In order to have peace and love, you must start with love between family members. Divorce has torn apart many families and has caused displacement of many children. Pray that your families are in accord with each other and do not let materialistic things come between you. Even within your countries, civil wars have torn people apart over their political differences. Divisions have been seen often even in religion between various sects and among various members. Keep in mind that it is the evil one stirring up dissension that causes many of your divisions. Pray, My people, for unity in all of your organizations and countries. It is only through love and generous compromise that you will keep peace. Search even for My peace among you which has a more lasting effect than your worldly peace. If there is not enough prayer for peace, your world could destroy itself."

Later, at Adoration, I could see a night scene and several people were standing and following some bright spots of moving light. Jesus said: "My people, I have given you messages and visions before about how your guardian angels are going to show you the way to the caves and safe havens. You again, are seeing the light of the angels and they will lead you to places of holy ground. Follow their lights to the places where I will feed you and cure all of your diseases and sicknesses. Even at the places of My caves, the blessed waters of the grotto will heal any of your sicknesses. You will see, this blessed healing will become more important to you as more epidemics of disease spread all over your land. Give thanks to God for all of the miraculous ways of protection that will be provided for you during the tribulation. Have no fear and trust in Me completely to lead your souls to Heaven. You may suffer persecution, but in the end, those souls following the Antichrist will have to suffer much more severe plagues on earth."

**Tuesday, May 5, 1998:**

After Communion, I could see a kneeler and below it a dark grotto of water. Jesus said: "My people, prayer in meditation is an important part of everyone's life. You remember many times when I went into the mountains or the desert to pray. This is your link with God to help restore your spiritual strength. Prayer is like an oasis where you are refreshed again spiritually in your soul. I have witnessed this to you in the Scriptures to give you an example of how to imitate Me. Before great events or after exhausting experiences, I was drawn to prayer to My Father for help. Remember again how I asked My disciples to pray with Me in the Garden of Gethsemane, right before I was to die. I ask you also to spend an hour with Me each day, so I can infuse My graces in you to strengthen you for your day's trials. Come to Me, My children, for My yoke is easy and My burden is light."

Later, at Adoration, I could see some beautiful flowers and then they turned black in color. Jesus said: **"My people, these flowers in beautiful array are like the souls of the people on earth. But when the Antichrist comes, he will mislead many souls that are not prepared for his coming. It is those souls that lose their way to Me by believing in the Antichrist, that are turning black to indicate their spiritual death. I am asking My faithful to take notice of this evil man and have nothing to do with him. Do everything to avoid his powers by going in to the rural areas away from the authorities. Do not watch him on TV or listen to his voice. He will have superhuman powers to mislead even some of My faithful. Guard yourself with your blessed sacramentals and seek My help to sustain you from his powers. My power will overshadow him, and those, faithful to Me, will have nothing to fear. Look on this as a spiritual battle for souls, and struggle to give example to even the lost souls. Your efforts to touch their souls may be their means of salvation."**

**Wednesday, May 6, 1998:**

After Communion, I could see some tall skyscrapers and a large platform was descending to the ground like an elevator. Jesus said: **"My people, the morality of your society has reached a low ebb. Your death culture continues to rule in causing abortions and other killings. You continue to warp the minds of My little ones with all manner of abuse. Your reverence, and even acknowledgment of Me in your lives, is only known among a few. I have brought down Sodom and Gomorrah for less than what you are doing. Your perversions of sex in heterosexual and homosexual unions are an abomination. I have been merciful to** man in allowing you time to amend your lives after many messages have been given to you. **But still many are not listening, nor are they making any attempts to purify their lives. My attempts to get your attention have fallen on deaf ears. I will try once again to get your attention through the next wave of storms and pestilence of insects, disease and fires. If you still do not come to your knees, I will send My warning among you to make you realize how your sins offend Me. The Devil will have one last gasp during your tribulation, and then all those evil ones will be chained in Hell. Remember that those condemned to Hell will suffer there for an eternity. Spare yourselves this grief by reaching out to Me in love. Grab on to Me as a lifesaver, for soon all of this world's evil will come to an end. My mercy has not been accepted, so My justice must cleanse the earth once and for all."**

Later, after Communion, I could see Mary dressed in white and behind her was a cross with a white cloth. Mary said: **"My dear children, I am happy for all of you that could come to honor me for this month of May. My Jesus has called me to be your mother through St. John, the Apostle, from Jesus' own lips. Jesus and I have our hearts joined as one. He leads you to Him through my intercession. Because we are so close, I give your petitions personally to my Son. He will answer your prayers according to His Will. Continue to offer up your Rosaries for My intentions. Prayers are needed for peace, to stop abortions, to pray for sinners, and to pray for the poor souls in Purgatory. When you have free time, spend as much time in prayer and doing things for my Son as you can. I love you all for listening to my call."**

### Thursday, May 7, 1998:

After Communion, I could see an ornate "E" for evil. Jesus said: **"My people, evil abounds in your world and anyone, who denies it, is a liar. You know by Adam's fall that you have inherited a weakness to sin. You should not be insulted to know that you are a sinner, but you should be open to accept this reality. It is for this reason that I came to die for your sins, and also it is why you are happy to celebrate My Resurrection. By**

My victory over sin, you have been enabled to have your sins forgiven and enter Heaven. What I have done for you is not a general absolution forever. Much like when you offend someone, you seek their forgiveness. So it is with Me. I have given you the Sacrament of Reconciliation to seek the forgiveness of your sins. Without seeking this forgiveness in sorrow for your sins, how can I forgive you? You cannot passively commit grave sins and think there is no consequence. When you love someone and offend them, you do everything to make it up to them. So it is with Me. If you truly love Me, you will be sorry to have offended Me. All sinners must repent of their sins throughout their whole lives. Without this contrition for sin, you are defying My forgiveness. Only pure souls can enter into Heaven. Unless you are purified by suffering and forgiveness, you will be languishing with your sins in Hell. Seek My graces in Confession, or seek My forgiveness in your own words for other faiths. Without repentance, no one can be saved."

Later, at the prayer group, I could see a crowd celebrating 'Mother Earth Day' with some gardens. Jesus said: "My people, do not worship the earth or the stars, or any other attributes of the earth. You have but one Creator in God and Him only should you worship. Do not let the New Age Movement and all of its earthly gods lead you astray. Order cannot come from chaos and it was by My Will that everything came into existence. I created the stars and the planets, the plants and the animals. Finally, I placed man on earth in My image. Follow the Bible in all of your origins, and you will see why I only am worthy of your homage."

I could see some pyramids and signs of the Egyptian Civilization. Jesus said: "My people, learn from the history of previous civilizations how to live your lives in accordance with My Commands. Those, who honored their God and had strong family relationships, were longer lasting. Many strong people failed by decay from within than by invaders. Your society has been strong because your forefathers based their laws on My laws. As your laws and behavior violate My laws, you are decaying as a world power. Follow My ways and hold on to your roots, and you will find strength to survive."

I could see some animals in your ads on TV selling things. Jesus said: **"My people, sometimes your animal craving of things of the world control you more than your inherited spiritual calling. You are so wrapped up in your instant gratification that you neglect to realize why you are here. You are all My creatures made to know, love and serve Me. Look at your spiritual body and see that you are here to follow My Will and not just your will. Coming to a love for My ways takes My grace and help which I will provide at your request. Share in My infinite love and you will have everything your soul desires."**

I could see St. Therese come and she reminded me of her roses that I saw several times during the week. St. Therese said: **"My little children, this is a beautiful time when nature is blooming in the flowers and the trees. This rebirth of new life is timed well around your celebration of Jesus' Resurrection. See this beauty of new life can come among all of your souls as you cast aside the darkness of your sins along with the dark winter. It is this joyous life in Jesus that I call all souls to come forward and experience. Free your souls from sin in His sacraments and your joy will be complete."**

I could see some Churches and their altars were disfigured with vandalism and graffiti. Jesus said: **"My people, your churches are decaying as your sins are piled one on another. As you defy My laws, many of your religious practices will be defiled. Soon your worship will only honor man's traditions instead of My own. Your worship will deteriorate into a blasphemy that will bring about the destruction of your churches. Follow My laws, no matter how unpopular you will be among your peers. You have to answer to Me first and not other men."**

I could see some large government buildings going into darkness. Jesus said: **"Your justice system is slowly stagnating to favor the rich and the powerful. Without money and a proper lawyer, those without much means are being robbed of what little they have. Those, who can pay for the best lawyers, are winning cases they do not justly deserve. This has not changed since My day, but it does not justify these injustices in your system. This is the area where your freedoms will gradually be taken away from you. Even if justice is not given in this world,** all of these thieves and murderers will have to answer to My justice that is true."

I could see a series of black, wide steps for a choir. Jesus said: "My people, you are seeing the evil ones in your society that are using satanic power to go higher in their stations in life. Many, who resort to killing and stealing, find ways to accumulate wealth and power. Those striving for only their own power and things are already repaid in this world. They will not live to experience My heavenly glory, for they are unworthy. See that these powers on the earth are used by Satan to carry out his mischief. In the end My power will cast all of this evil lot into Hell where their pride will rot with them in the flames."

### Friday, May 8, 1998:

After Communion, I could see some nearly empty pews at a daily Mass. Jesus said: "My people, those, that come to daily Mass and Communion, are My special faithful who come out of a true sense of love and not just a duty. Daily Mass people understand the extra graces and help from My Blessed Sacrament that can help them through life's daily trials. Many of these souls are dedicated to following My Will, rather than their own. It takes a positive decision of your will to desire to make the sacrifice of time and effort to get to daily Mass. These faithful have a special place in My heart, and they will be guarded and encouraged in their faith. I would encourage those who can to attend either an early or later daily Mass, and you will be greatly rewarded for following Me. You will have an extra measure of hearing My words of Scripture, along with the priest's homily. Each day you can place My words into your daily actions. Your joyful spirit can then be shared with your co-workers."

Later, at Adoration, I could see God the Father all in gold and He had a cross behind Him. God the Father said: "I AM is showing you the Cross that My Son had to bear for your sins. As you have been reading about St. John's Gospel, Jesus has told you how the two of Us are One. He leads you to Me, as He is suffering for your sins. This Resurrection, that you are celebrating, represents Jesus' greatest miracle before men. His power comes from Our Union and it defies even Satan's power. So trust in

Jesus for all the help that you will need in your coming trials. All of the plans, that I have for man on the earth, will be fulfilled in My time. I did many things to protect My people in the past in the desert, so believe that I will continue to protect My faithful. You will see great events come about that will fulfill the Book of Revelation. Have trust in My protection, no matter how much the evil spirits and evil men will taunt you."

**Saturday, May 9, 1998:**

After Communion, I could see a nun in her habit playing an organ. Jesus said: **"My people, I am emphasizing today the need for your prayers for vocations to the priesthood and the sisterhood. Without these ministers coming forward, it will continue to be difficult to provide for My Church. Pray also for those accepting these vocations and their teachers. Many vocations have been turned away and discouraged by those at the seminaries. Pray also that these teachers give proper training to instill My love and My Word in these new candidates. Many schools have not been teaching My Word, but their own ideas of what pleases them. My future priests need a proper grounding in the sacraments and a good prayer life. Without the true teachings of the Apostles, these new priests could mislead My faithful in false teachings. Already, My priests are not encouraging people enough to have their sins forgiven in Confession. Without proper teaching of the faithful, many will fall to Satan."**

Later, at Adoration, I could see a wilderness scene in the woods through the spokes of a bicycle wheel. There was a sense of being pursued in persecution. Jesus said: **"My people, have no fear of the tribulation time. This is a time of purification and testing, but those, who follow My ways, have nothing to be afraid of. Many souls are Christian in name only, so when this persecution comes, it will test how much you love Me. I was willing to die for each one of you. Do you love Me enough to die for My Name's sake if you are put to the test? I will give My faithful the grace of what to say and the grace to endure any suffering, even if you are to be martyred. Those, who live during the tribulation and are faithful, will be rewarded with My Era of Peace and will not have to suffer purgatory. It is better to suffer your** purgatory in the tribulation, than to suffer real purgatory in the next life. Those, who take the easy way out by accepting the Antichrist, will have to suffer a hell on earth and real hell for an eternity. You will not escape suffering, but you will enjoy the beauty of My glory in Heaven if you stand by My Name. Pray for spiritual strength for the souls here, that they may see the light and join the side of My glory. For those, who love Me in all of this testing, your reward will far outweigh any temporary suffering you may have to endure."

**Sunday, May 10, 1998:** (Mother's Day)

After Communion, I could see some construction rods and other building materials. Jesus said: **"My people, I am asking you this Mother's Day to build up My Kingdom in My Church. For every new life that comes into your family, you need to assure them of My sacraments and bring them into My Church membership. Even those souls already in My fold need tending as well. Living souls are never the same. You are either improving in your faith or on the decline. It is important to be joyous and encouraging others to increase their love for God and neighbor. Always be working to improve your prayer life and give good example for others to improve as well. By your frequenting My sacraments, you are giving a model life to show others how to improve their lives. When you bring souls back to Me, they need to see you constantly witnessing to your faith."**

Later, at Adoration, I could see a building with darkened windows to indicate a secret meeting of significance was going on. Jesus said: **"My people, this G7 meeting of your largest financial countries is about to trigger some future events. These evil men are continuing to plot the takeover of your world in readiness for the Antichrist to take charge. Wars or threats of war will be used to scare the people into giving their leaders emergency powers. This will be coupled with manipulated monetary instabilities to throw your markets into a panic. All of this will be a planned means to have the evil ones gain control of your world. They know by certain means that their time is running out. Be prepared My faithful for some significant events to happen soon. Remember to be prepared in your soul by confession** and physically with your sacramentals and physical needs to leave when events show you it is time. I have told you the warning happens first, followed by the pope's exile and the Mark of the Beast being demanded of everyone. Have no fear, but pray for courage and My protection. Follow only Me and never give in to belief in anyone else."

**Monday, May 11, 1998:**

After Communion, I could see a large 'A' to represent alpha and omega. Jesus said: **"My son, when My disciples were praised, they did not want to take any glory for themselves. So it is with you in any way that you may receive confirmations. These signs are given for those around you, as you understand the significance of My work in you. But do not use these things to make yourself look good in men's eyes. Remember to continue to give Me all the praise for all that is happening. No matter how much people want to patronize you, remind them again that it is through My power that all is received. To keep humble and peaceful in your prayer life, that is My calling for you. Speak out My words and never credit yourself with anything, since you are all nothing before Me. I love all of My faithful and I am encouraging My messengers that I will watch out for your protection at all times."**

Later, at Adoration, I could see a path outside and then the open jaws of a wolf. Jesus said: **"My people, beware in this world of the various evil spirits who are like ravenous wolves ready to devour any unsuspecting soul. Many do not realize the dangers lurking in all of the distractions of your world. Some are even drawn into satanic cults in search of power and riches. My people, call on the protection of your guardian angels and My help to keep your souls from the clutches of Satan and all of his minions. As the evil ones are coming to the height of their power, you will need Me more in guarding your soul. Without seeking My help, you will surely be lost. See that you are in a battle for souls and be always on guard for your soul's protection as well as the danger present for other souls. By your example of prayer and your sacramentals, show others how to protect themselves from the evil spirits. Tell people what to avoid** in order to be saved. Seek the power of the Holy Spirit in chasing the evil ones from you. You have been given the tools to save your soul and others. Strive at all times to save souls, for you will be tested beyond what you have seen up to now. Have no fear, for with Me, you will be saved."

Tuesday, May 12, 1998:

After Communion, I could see a dock for a small boat. Jesus said: "My people, those, who go out like St. Paul and spread the good news, have a special place in My heart. It is not easy to bring My Word to total strangers, even when it is a difficult message. Those disciples, who do missionary work, are always at the mercy of the people they visit. Some may welcome you, while others may reject you. Many opposed My teaching because they had to sacrifice in changing their lives. That is why the Gospel message is not always popular. Still, even if people object to My Word, you must continue to spread the good news of My Resurrection. Accept what others provide for you and be ready for some suffering. You will be persecuted and tested, since saving souls has a cost associated with it. These souls need to be changed by prayer and fasting. Satan does not give up without a fight. Just as St. Paul returned often to the cities that he started his work, it is necessary to maintain the stability of even the souls you have brought back to Me. You have to be just as persistent as the evil one fighting you."

Later, at Adoration, I could see someone putting a table together for an underground Mass. Jesus said: "My people, again I am asking you to gather your things for the Mass. You will need bread, wine, books, vessels and candles. You would be advised also to befriend a priest loyal to Me that would have a place to stay. Celebrate the Mass as long as you can. Then you will have to carry My Consecrated Host from place to place to preserve My True Presence among you. You will realize how precious the Mass is when it will be difficult to attend one. My faithful will be persecuted by the Antichrist and his agents. They will hate those who love Me. Protect yourself with Confession, while you have the priests, and protect yourself with your blessed sacramentals. The power of good will prevail even against the evil ones. I will see to your protection when you call on Me for help. Continue to have no fear when you have faith in My victory. My triumph will follow quickly after the evil one has gained power. Your suffering will be brief and then you will share in the glory of My Era of Peace on earth."

**Wednesday, May 13, 1998:**
After Communion, I could see some bleachers for a sports game side by side with some pews in a Church. Jesus said: **"My people, you have placed your sports in direct competition with My Sunday services that you should be attending. There is also a contrast here in that you should be worshiping Me and not the gods of sports. Exercise and gaming has its place, but it should not become such a focus as a god in itself. In addition, My day of rest has been violated again by all of your games on Sunday. Instead of prayer and meditation on Sunday, your media has hyped these games again to occupy your time with more worldly pursuits. Take stock of how you spend your time and think more of doing things for Me than any of your selfish interests."**

**Thursday, May 14, 1998:** (St. Matthias)
After Communion, I could see a Bible and the rest of the Church was being destroyed. Jesus said: **"My people, I have given this message many times before to prepare you for the time of your persecution. Many of your churches will be destroyed as the tribulation of the Antichrist comes upon you. You may think that this can never happen, but persecution of My Church is going on even now in many parts of the world. Evil will have its day for a moment during the Antichrist's brief reign. This time has been foretold in the Bible and it has to happen by My plan. All souls will be tested at that time, so listen to My plea for your spiritual preparation in Confession. Without calling on My help, you will be lost. This will be a test of everyone's faith in Me. Those, who seek My help and that of their guardian angels, will be protected and they should have no fear. My power will overcome Satan and the Antichrist as you will see My triumph cast all of these evil men and evil spirits into Hell. Look to My victory and beyond your brief moment of suffering."**

Later, at the prayer group, I could see an Egyptian statue of a god and there was a rumbling and shimmering of that statue. Jesus said: **"My people, I have shown you before that evil power will be raised up again from the evil gods of long ago in Egypt. These powers have remained dormant for many years, but when the Antichrist assumes power, many demons will be unleashed on the earth. I have told you to prepare for a spiritual battle with an evil that you have yet to experience. Have no fear since I will overpower all of the demons fighting for souls. You will need My help and your sacramentals for your protection."**

I could see a bright shining light in the sky different from your sun and moon. Jesus said: **"My people, I have warned you many times to observe the signs in your skies for some future events. You have been observing several comets and other signs in other star systems, as your technology has helped you to view them. These are omens of the coming tribulation and the eventual great chastisement which will deliver My triumph. My justice is coming soon to cleanse the evil from the earth. You will eventually even view the coming of this chastisement, but nothing will prevent My triumph from happening."**

I could see some strong sunlight coming in some windows from the top of a Church roof. Jesus said: **"My people, there will be a great celebration in My Church before the coming of the Antichrist. Many will be cheering your current pope for awhile. Then evil will prevail over Rome for a short time. It will be My triumph later that will usher in My renewed earth when all My faithful will rejoice in My love. My victory will be so overwhelming that no one will ever doubt My power is complete."**

I could see Jesus sitting in the tomb with a great light about Him. Jesus said: **"My people, I am speaking great words of faith through My Holy Shroud. When I died and was Resurrected, the signs of this event were captured in the Holy Shroud. More souls will have their faith enhanced when the evidence of My Resurrection becomes fully known. Believe in Me as your Savior, since I have opened Heaven's Gates, and I show you the Gate to Heaven. Many souls have photographed this gate. Signs of My glory abound and you will see signs greater than these."**

I could see some rockets taking off. Jesus said: **"My people, your leaders are confusing in their speech since they have double standards. You chastise other nations for developing missiles and bombs when you have done and are doing the same thing. The more weapons your technology develops, brings you closer one day to try and use them. Pray for peace and that these nuclear devices are never used in war."**

I could see a tower of Babel in the shape of a large stone pyramid. Jesus said: **"My people, man has built many buildings and civilizations which he thought were indestructible. For each time man has made himself a god in his power, I have brought him low for his worship of idols. You have raised up technology and your materialism as your god. Soon I will bring you to your knees and all of your possessions will be dashed to the ground in utter destruction. Give praise and glory to Me only. All those, worshiping anyone or anything other than Me, will be chained in Hell."**

I could see a great dove representing the Holy Spirit. The Holy Spirit said: **"I am the Spirit of Love and you will soon be celebrating My infusion into the Apostles and Mary. See that My power is among all of you in the temple of your spirit. My love is ever present among you. Call on My gifts at any time and I will bestow any graces on you that you will need. Ask of My abundant graces and they will be granted to those who are faithful to God's Commands. Rejoice in My feast at Pentecost for you will see events unfolding according to God's plan."**

### Friday, May 15, 1998:

After Communion, I could look down and see some people walking on a white colored background, while others were on a black background. Jesus said: **"My people, you need to take special care in making moral decisions. Many people, given the same set of facts, tell a different story. You interpret things differently based on your understanding of the facts. Many of your history books have been slanted according to certain people's agendas. This is why it is important to abide by My Church's teaching authority to base your moral thinking. Forming a proper conscience to know right from wrong starts with an un-**

derstanding of natural law and My Commandments interpreted by the Church. You need to also pray to the Holy Spirit for discernment of serious issues. Making your moral decisions, based on your own understanding, may lead some to error, if they are inclined to take the easy way out. Do not rely on just feelings for such decisions. Test your reasoning with your Catechism, the Church's beliefs and My Scriptures to better understand your moral options. When you seek My understanding, you will be more enlightened than with just your own interpretation."

Later, at St. Margaret Mary Adoration, Harrisburg, Pa., I could see some spires of a Church. Jesus said: "**My people, I am asking you to build up My Church by loving one another. Start with your priest and do everything to encourage him and help him in his ministry. Even if you may disagree with things that he does, bear with it as he supplies you with the graces of Mass and the sacraments. Unless he does things directly against My Church, then speak to him in a kind way of your concern. If it is of a serious enough nature, then address your concern to the Bishop. Do not gossip about one another and love even those you dislike and those who persecute you. By your love, you will help to unite My Church rather than cause division. When each of you share My love with one another, you will frustrate Satan's desire to divide you with hate and accusations. Fight this battle against evil that strives to divide you. The more you pray to strengthen each other, the stronger I will be among you in your parish. With everyone working to please Me, you will be less focused on criticism. I pour out My love on all of you and I wish that you would share this love with each other.**"

### Saturday, May 16, 1998:

At Holy Name of Jesus Church near Harrisburg, Pa., I could see a wooden Church with oval shaped domes coming to a point as in the Eastern Rite Church. Jesus said: "**My people, I spoke to you of unity in your individual churches. Today, I want you to pray for the unification of the Roman Rite and the Eastern Rite churches. You have seen my Pope son, John Paul II make some overtures to unite these churches. Although there were divisions in the past, you still believe in My Real Presence. It is** only pride and a reluctance to accept each other that stands in the way of this unification. In My new Era of Peace you will all be joined as one people with no more divisions of Satan. Even now you can pray that these man-made divisions could be healed. You are all brothers and sisters through Me, why do you insist on keeping these barriers between each other? If you are to fight the evil one, you must join together in a united front."

Later, at St. Margaret Mary's Adoration near Harrisburg, Pa., I could see a roof soffit where a light fixture was torn off. Then I looked down a city street and there were huge crevasses from an earthquake in the street. Jesus said: **"My people, you will begin to witness an increase in earthquakes as a result of an increased solar wind from the sun. Massive eruptions on the sun will be affecting your communications and brownouts will occur with this increase in solar activity. Many signs will be happening soon in your skies to give further witness of the coming End Times. As more events occur, people will start to wonder why these things are happening with such an increase in frequency. Some will be struck with fear, but My faithful should be joyous that My triumph is soon to come. Do not despair that these times have not come yet. Everything happens according to My plan and My time. Many messages have been foretold of these warnings of cataclysmic activity. Once these things are put into motion, many will be shocked into panic, because they did not believe in My prophecies. Your time is short before the tribulation will be upon you. Believe and prepare for this evil that will reach a height that you could not believe possible. With prayer and a request for My help, you will be protected from evil in many miraculous ways."**

### Sunday, May 17, 1998:

At St. Ferdinand's Church, Cranberry, Pa. after Communion I could see a stairway to Heaven and many people were on their way to judgment. Jesus said: **"My people, I ask your love at all times, as I love you with an infinite love. The priest was right to compare someone famous with one of common background to emphasize that all of you are equal before Me. You are all equal at all times, not just at the judgment. I love each of you with the** same love. As you compare worldly renown, I am taken with a person's spiritual riches that they have stored up in life. Without Me you are nothing. So seek My help, so I can lead you to follow My Will. Many of My saints have shown you by their example how to live a loving life of following My Will. It is seeking to live in My Divine Will of perfection that every soul is drawn, but few follow completely. Reach out to perfect your life as much as possible, because your stay here is very short. See that one day when you die, you will be standing in this line to face judgment. Prepare now spiritually for the day of your entry into the next life. It will be by your deeds and how much you love Me and your neighbor that you will be judged."

Later, at Adoration, I could see some airplane wheels turning. Jesus said: "My son, you are being tested in many ways, but do not be discouraged. My grace goes with you to continue your travel to speak out in My Name. As you see these wheels going forward, continue in your work for as long as you can. Your time for spreading My Word is short and you need to take advantage of every opportunity to save souls. You have been graced with My understanding and My Word in your heart. Few souls have the courage and the gifts that I have given you. That is why you must work hard to bring the Word of My Kingdom to those with an open heart. Many who read the messages are touched in their hearts with the extent of My love poured out on everyone. Those, willing to accept My love and seek the forgiveness of their sins in Confession, will surely be saved and protected. You will find many persecutions coming upon you and those around you from the evil ones who do not want My Word of light and truth to reach My little ones. Continue to pray for your persecutors and for those helping you to spread My Word. Without continued prayer and fasting, your words will fall on deaf ears. You will always have to struggle and suffer to deliver souls to My fold."

**Monday, May 18, 1998:**

After Communion, I could see a small cross on each of the pews in a Church. Jesus said: "My people, each of you in the pews must carry your own crosses, if you are to be My disciples. As you look at the many faces in church, you see how each of you are called to suffer in various ways. Some may have a cross of bad health and have the opportunity to offer their sufferings up for saving souls. Others may be called to be prayer warriors to balance the evil on My scales of justice. Still others may be called to evangelize or even prophecy My Word to those willing to listen. You all are different and are called to help My living Church. Do not refuse your calling, but bear what you are asked as I carried My cross to Calvary. Those, who follow My Will and listen to My Call, will store great spiritual riches for the day they come to Heaven."

At Adoration, I could see a cup with Our Lord's Most Precious Blood inside of it. On top of the cup I could see a beautiful dark red rose and St. Therese standing next to it. St. Therese said: **"My little one, take a long look at Jesus' cup of life that He had to give up in order to save all of humanity. Remember His words in the garden when He gave his consent to His Father. 'Yet not as I will, but as Thou willest.' These are the same words asked of each soul. Are each of you prepared to offer your life up to God if you are put to the test for the sake of His Name? It is this full belief in Jesus that would cause you to say yes without any hesitation. This readiness to die for your Savior shows Him how true your love is for Him and how much faith you have in His Word. Some will be martyred in the tribulation, but your reward of Resurrection in glorified bodies will be your reward. This is why those, who are true disciples of Jesus, are always at peace and have no fear of losing their lives for His sake."**

**Tuesday, May 19, 1998:**

After Communion, I could see a bright light coming from some pews in the Church. Jesus said: **"My people, this light in the pews is to indicate how one day My disciples will see their glorified bodies. This life is a constant struggle with the stress of the workplace and the effects of evil in all facets of your life. Daily you are faced with distractions and curiosities which take you away from your prayer life. To stay focused on Me, despite these things around you, takes a grace of faith and perseverence. If you desire to be with Me in Heaven in a glori-**

fied body, you must pay the price of suffering and endurance in this life of testing."

Later, at Adoration, I could look down on three babies all around a table. Jesus said: "My people, when you look down on these babies, you are looking at the number one target of Satan. If he can have you kill the babies for him, you have done his dirty work for him. Satan wishes to eliminate all of mankind in any devious way, because he so hates man by My becoming one of you. Do everything in your power by prayer, love and deeds to stop abortions. Also, in the same manner pray for all of the children who are being abused physically and spiritually. Watch over your own children and grandchildren, so you can protect their souls from Satan's attack in sex, drugs and other perversions. The children are the most vulnerable, so you need to pray and struggle to shield them from Satan's venom. Guard their minds from the deceptions on your TVs and movies. Protect them as much as possible from evil day care people and evil babysitters. You need to pay attention to everything that can lead them away from Me. On the other side, protect them by giving them Blessed Sacramentals as Rosaries, Scapulars, and Crucifixes. Read them the Scriptures, take them to Mass and take them to My Sacraments. By your good example lead all of the children to a strong faith in Me. Satan is very strong now and you need to work especially hard to save your souls and the souls of the children."

**Wednesday, May 20, 1998:**

After Communion, I could see a tombstone in the shape of the gateway to Heaven. Jesus said: "My people, many people think of death as something far off in the future with no present significance. I assure you that life is a very thin string which could be ended for you in many different ways. Many people die each day and come to judgment totally unprepared. This tombstone represents a doorway to the next life that is a transition from this testing place to the present now. Your spirit is immortal and you will live on forever. It is by what you do in life that determines your final destination. When you think of how long eternity is, you would think more would prepare better to face this fact. You have been created to know, love and serve Me in Heaven and on earth. By many people's actions, they think they were only created for this earthly life. Everyone should be prepared to die everyday. I have asked you to be on guard for your soul's protection, because I will come for you like a thief in the night. Remember you are created for My glory and not for yours. If you desire to accept Me and wish to be with Me in Heaven, then have your soul ready at all times to receive Me. This is why frequent Confession is necessary to keep your soul free from sin at all times. You must see yourself as a sinner and desire to have your sins forgiven. To repent of your sins means that you are sorry for having offended Me and you will try not to sin again. The human condition makes you weak to sin, so you have to struggle to follow My Will. Never despair over your sins, but keep your soul cleansed, so when I do call you home, your spiritual life will be in order to receive Me."

**Thursday, May 21, 1998:** (Ascension Thursday)

After Communion, I saw a dark room and later Jesus gave His farewell. Jesus said: **"My people, My disciples were elated with My Resurrection and they became comfortable with My appearances. They became saddened when I had to leave, but I told them that the Holy Spirit would instill them to carry out My mission. Many of My present day disciples have not seen Me, but you have been gifted with My popes and priests to lead you in faith to My sacraments. As you prepare for the coming feast of Pentecost, think of how the Apostles must have felt in the upper room after I left them. There are times in your lives when you must have felt lonely without anyone to help you. Call on My help and that of the Holy Spirit at any time and We will come to your aid. Do not despair in your sins and weaknesses, but come to Confession where your sins can be forgiven and your spirits lifted up once again. Do not be sad, but lift yourselves up to rejoice in My victory over sin and death. You have all reason to be joyful in My love for you and the love of the Holy Spirit within you. Turn this dark room of fear into a new bright room of faith and hope in My triumph over this world."**

Later, at the prayer group, I could see a blind man leaning against a pillar of the Church. Jesus said: **"My people, you can give alms to the poor, but even more important you are to share your love and faith with everyone. No matter who requests your help, you need to recognize My presence in each soul. Do not belittle the downtrodden, even if they have caused their own problems. Pray with everyone and do not reject My Presence in anyone. By showing your love for even those you dislike, you will gain riches in Heaven."**

I could see some large jars of water as those that Jesus changed into wine. Jesus said: **"My people, I have reminded you of My miracle at Cana that was performed at My mother's request. I will answer your requests through your heavenly mother as well. This changing of substances is an example to you how I will provide for your needs during the tribulation. Have faith in My miracles and you will see them performed before your eyes. Do not doubt My power, but believe in the fulfillment of My promises to watch over you."**

I could see a crucifix laying on the ground next to a river. Jesus said: **"My people, you have seen many images in your Easter season and one of them is water. When you are Baptized with water, your sins are washed away. When you were Baptized as an infant, others spoke for you in denying the evil one. As you grow older, you need to repeat your Baptismal vows with true meaning. If you truly love Me, you will deny Satan and all of his lies and promises of this world's distractions. You are in the world, but not of the world, when you accept Me as your Savior."**

I could see some prison bars. Jesus said: **"My people, have mercy on those in prison and pray for their conversion. I have asked you to visit the sick and the prisoners. As you look on their suffering in the loss of their freedom, think of the days when man's laws will condemn you for protecting the unborn or for believing in My Name. There will come a day when you do not worship the Antichrist, that evil men will torture and martyr you for My Name's sake. Never give allegiance to any-one but Me, even if it means losing your life."**

I could see Jesus with a crown of thorns and then a man with some electrical device on his head. Jesus said: **"My people, in My** suffering of the crown of thorns, this was to cleanse all of the evil thoughts in the minds of men. In your new age of the end times, man will heap electronic brain washing on those victims refusing to follow the New World Order. You will see electrical devices torture men with shocks to force them against their own will. Do not take any chips in your body or you will be controlled through them. You will see torture and inhumane acts done to those not obeying the evil one."

I could see someone in Western clothes that abused the Indians. Jesus said: **"My people, just as the new settlers took the land and freedom from the Indians, your new evil rulers will separate you from your possessions. Do not think that you will be comfortable in the days of the tribulation. You will suffer to believe in My Name, but your suffering will be brief. Those, who worship the Antichrist and refuse to accept Me, will suffer worse punishments both on earth and in Hell. A brief suffering for Me is far better than eternal punishment from the demons and the flames of Hell."**

I could see a young girl as Mary. Mary said: **"You, my children, are seeing the flames of the Holy Spirit over me and the Apostles at Pentecost. Our Lord had granted me many privileges even before this grace of the Holy Spirit. I was protected from sin even before my birth and thereafter. It was the grace of the Holy Spirit that conceived Jesus in my womb. The flame of love, that I received, was a culmination of graces to give myself and the Apostles courage to proclaim my Son's teachings. Rejoice in your Sacraments, given by Jesus, to strengthen you in your faith against the evil one."**

**Friday, May 22, 1998:**

After Communion, I could see a priest dressed in his vestments. Jesus said: **"My people, treasure the faithful priests who will be with Me after the schism in the Church. The Antipope will try and mislead My people and the clergy. It will take a strong willed priest to not take the easy way out. There will be a division over following John Paul II or not, and the priests will have to decide which side to go with. The Antipope will be working with the Masons and the Antichrist to destroy My Church.**

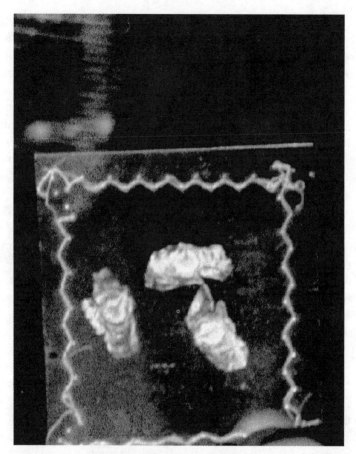

*Miraculous Manna from the Philippines*

My remnant underground church will be faithful to My laws and they will protect My Real Presence in the proper Consecration of the Mass. When you cannot find a Mass, you will have My angels bring you spiritual communion with My miraculous manna. Pray for strength and discernment to follow My Will and not this false witness or the Antichrist."

Later, at Adoration, I could see the Statue of Liberty and it turned into an ugly tyrant. Jesus said: **"My people, you have obtained your freedoms through My help and your own blood on the battle fields. You have even fought in your Bill of Rights for freedom of worship. You have placed Me in your documents as** a right purpose to live by My laws. In recent years, your morals have decayed to the point where My Ten Commandments are put out of your public buildings. You have declared atheism as your religion by your separation of church and state. You even have not allowed prayer in your schools. You write your own laws permitting abortions, euthanasia and homosexual unions. You see the image of the beast that you will be forced to worship. Evil is having its way for a moment, but your country will witness its own ruin brought about by your actions. Because you have violated My laws and you worship your materialism more than Me, I will bring you to wallow in your sins and your possessions will be stripped from you. Your nation will face massive destruction and takeover as a chastisement for your sins. I will come to the aid of My faithful and guide them in this tribulation. Those, who refuse to accept Me, will be punished severely both on earth and in Hell. Choose to follow Me now or you will surely be lost."

### Saturday, May 23, 1998:

After Communion, I could see some unusual radio waves coming up from below the ground. Jesus said: **"My people, this vision is to show you that evil spirits from below will control electrical signals with microwaves. The television images of the Antichrist will control the minds of all those viewing them through the power of suggestion. By the use of satellites, large antennas, and microchips, the evil men will control many people all over the world. Your money and your jobs will be under total control of these evil men. Buying and selling with the chips will be under their control. In order to avoid this control, I am asking you not to take any chips in your body and not to worship anyone but Me. The Antichrist will reign for a time, but My triumph will overpower all of the evil one's designs to control men. All of these evil spirits and evil men will be chained in Hell and then My peace will reign supreme without any evil influence. In the new Era of Peace you will no longer have to suffer any trials, but My love and peace will dominate the world. Have faith and hope in My Word and My faithful will enjoy this time of My triumphant glory."**

Later, at Adoration, I could see some large submarines with missiles. Jesus said: **"My people, you are familiar with the battles of World War II, but you will be faced with a surprise attack that you could not imagine. When your troops are cut back and the remainder sent abroad for trumped up reasons, you will be primed for a takeover by the United Nations troops on your soil. Your enemies right now are the Masons and the One World people, who have been planning your takeover for years. Your president and your Congress have sold the American people over to the One World evil forces of the New World Order. You have taken Me out of your lives, so now the chastisements of My justice must fall. The Antichrist and his forces will cheer their victory for a moment. Then My triumph will wipe away all the evil men and evil spirits. Their power is nothing against Me. I will then dispatch all of these evil men to eternal punishment in Hell. The demons will be chained in Hell and My faithful will rejoice to be in a new Era of My Peace. I will bring My victory about with one blow of My hand and everyone will bow on bended knee to My almighty power. Have no fear My faithful, for My victory was never in doubt. All you need is prayer and My help, and you will endure this trial with faith. I am asking all men to listen to My call for souls. Accept Me as your Savior, and you will have no worries. You must be tested, but your testing will be brief. Believe in My Word and eternal life with Me will be assured."**

### Sunday, May 24, 1998:

After Communion, I could see a large bright room with sunlight on the ceiling. There was a large crown and then I saw Mary as in the picture from Medjugorje. Mary said: **"My dear son, I am reminding you of your call here in Medjugorje and how the Lord asked you to reform your life. In order to preach His message, you must be on your guard at all times from the evil one's distractions. Devote your time to the Lord's mission in all that you do. Continue to resolve yourself to keep your soul guarded from things that consume your time and are not of God. You have been graced with more time and you need to plan it wisely for His glory. Continue to encourage people back** to the Lord in your evangelistic efforts. This is truly everyone's calling to save souls from Hell. This will be one of everyone's responsibilities at each of your judgments. Remind everyone that you meet to pray for My intentions and repent of their sins in Confession."

Later, at Adoration, I could see a house with some offices of authority. Jesus said: "**My people, you have tiny minds, because you only think in terms of worldly powers. You worry and fear the End Times for all of its destruction. I tell you not to be afraid, because I am always present. Did you doubt that I would use My absolute power to chain Satan at My Will? Many have talked of dates of future events, but I have told you that I would bring about My glory in My own time directed by the Father. Believe in Me and you will see these days of glory that all of My faithful will experience. Lead your lives in accordance with God's plan for you and you will live for My victory that will be claimed over all of mankind. So rejoice in the joy that My power is supreme and all the evil spirits in the world are subject to following My Will. I love all of you so much, and I want you to know that I will not leave you alone in this tribulation.**"

**Monday, May 25, 1998:** (Memorial Day)

After Communion, I could see some weapons and then a gasoline truck. Jesus said: "**My people, your country has made itself so dependent on foreign oil, that at the next war in the Middle East, you could see shortages appear. Your fuel reserves will be cut back and your leaders will use this reason to involve you in alliances that will eventually draw you into war. Your country has such a ravenous appetite for fuel, energy and comforts, that your people will give in to these commitments. Your troops will be spread so thin, that your country will be vulnerable to attack. You have become so soft and reliant on your weapons, that your shadow of weakness will expose your demise when these defenses will be stripped from you.**"

Later, at Adoration, I could see the outline and shadow of a ship at sea. There was a sense that all the people on board came into a different state of conscientiousness. Jesus said: "**My people, this vision is a witness of what it will be like at the time of the** warning. All of these souls recognized that they were in a different state of life than they were used to. It is as if they were suspended in limbo out of time. During this experience, each soul will come face to face with Me as at your judgment. You will see all of your life flashed before you and you will know true right from wrong as I would see your actions. You will know how your life stands with Me as if you were to die right now. By a miracle of My grace, all of these souls will then return to your original state of life as you know it. You will remember vividly all of your life's experiences to the least detail. Now you will be faced with the true condition of your soul as I would see it. Many will be in a state of shock to understand how evil you have been. You will understand more fully about your purpose in life in this place of testing. Some will change their lives and seek forgiveness of their sins. My faithful must be available to lead these souls to Me in Confession. Other souls will convince themselves that this was only an illusion and they will refuse to change their evil ways. These are the souls of those condemned to Hell. Pray for these souls for a change of heart or they will be lost. I am revealing this experience to you because the time of My warning draws close. Prepare your souls now with Confession, prayer, and fasting and your experience will be less severe than someone in serious sin."

**Tuesday, May 26, 1998:** (St. Phillip Neri)
After Communion, I could see a casket of a saint. Jesus said: **"My people, all of My saints have come to know My Will and have followed it. Look to the saints as your examples in life, because they witnessed to men by their lives how to live the Gospel. It is good for all of you to see also that living a saintly life is not impossible even in today's world. These souls do not seek notoriety, but they are satisfied enough to do My Will. One lesson you should learn is that obedience to My laws and those over you is very important. Prayer and fasting are also a part of a holy life. It should be in all of your interests to strive to imitate the saints and live with that inspiration to do everything for Me. When you consecrate your lives to Me, you are formally directing all of your actions as prayers. Continue to**

struggle everyday to live life to the fullest for My glory, and one day you can claim to be a saint with Me in Heaven."

Later, at Adoration, I could see something in space spinning out of control. Jesus said: "**My people, you have recently seen one of your communications satellites go awry causing a loss in service to many. You pride yourselves on your electronic comforts, but it does not take much to strip you of these comforts. Given some major disturbances on the sun or a shower of meteors, and your many satellites become more at risk. The more satellites that you send into orbit increases the risk of an incident to cause a malfunction. Do not be surprised as some of these comforts may be stripped from you. Many things you do are vulnerable to the elements of nature disrupting them. You will see an increase in these problems as you depend more on your technology than on Me. Man-made things are made for eventual failure. Things that I create will last as long as I will them to last. Put your faith and trust in the One who loves you, for these inventions are cold and destined for destruction. See that this life is imperfect in its means of decay and being tried by time. Your souls and the spiritual things will last forever. Point your focus on those things of Divine origin, and you will be rewarded with everlasting life with Me in Heaven.**"

**Wednesday, May 27, 1998:**

After Communion, I could see a light shining off a stone and then a mixed texture of a flat stone. Jesus said: "**My people, life is a mysterious blend of body and spirit. When the spirit is present, life teems with activity. Yet, once death comes over the body and the spirit leaves, the body decays back into the elements it was made of. You need to look at life in the body in awe of the beauty of creation. If more people took time to discover the uniqueness of each soul, you would better appreciate the gift of each life. People are so taken up with their material possessions that they do not take time to understand the workings of the spirit of each life. It is this spirit in each human being which represents the immortal character of your soul. The spirit is that part of you that will live forever and it is that part that leaves the body to come to judgment. You should treat life as**

something sacred and not anything you can discard at your whim. Every life is one of My creations and it is made into existence by the Holy Spirit. Again, you should be concerned with the destination of your spirit, for it was not meant to be on earth forever. Every creation has been made for My greater honor and glory. That is why it is proper to return praise and glory to the source of all life. Give thanks to Me for every day that you are alive. Even more, treat each life as precious, because its value is more than you can express in wealth or possessions. Each life has this value instilled in it because it is the image of the Creator reflected in each soul. Because of Adam's fall, your time here is very short. So appreciate this gift of life and see that your purpose is to know, love and serve Me at all times."

**Thursday, May 28, 1998:** (The Visitation Mass for 25th Anniversary of the Prayer Group)

After Communion, I could see Mary come dressed in white and blue. Mary said: **"My dear children, I am happy to cherish all of your prayer group for your faithfulness to praying my Rosary. Your prayers are needed more than ever for my intentions. If you have one message tonight, it is one of service that I** am asking of you for your neighbor. You have seen me assist Elizabeth and you have seen my Son wash the feet of the Apostles. By your corporal works of mercy, you are filling your hands with spiritual gifts. Always be willing to help your neighbor in need and you will be helping my Son in His Mystical Body."

Later, at the prayer group, I could see Jesus on the cross and then a large flaming circle, that was overhead, came down out of Heaven. Jesus said: **"My people, after I died for you on the Cross, I did not leave you orphans. As you are about to celebrate Pentecost, look on this halo of fire as the flame of the Holy Spirit resting over each of you. The Holy Spirit is in each one of you, so call on His flaming love to give you courage and all of the gifts of the Holy Spirit. Inspired by His grace, you can have faith in abundance."**

I could see a crucifix and it was being torn apart. Jesus said: **"My people, I have given you My Holy Sacramentals and still many refuse to have them in the homes, buildings and churches. My Crucifix is a sign of your own suffering that everyone must go through to reach Heaven. To deny My Cross is to deny the work that each of you must do for My glory. Raise the Cross with My Body up high, for in this seeming defeat lies My victory over Satan."**

I could see a ball of light in the sun and it shown down on a young child. Jesus said: **"My people, look on this little child as the light of My truth falls down on the children. Do not block this light from reaching the children. Everyone should be open to accept Me into their lives. I am the light of life that places love in your hearts. Teach the children how to come to Me so that they may have the same fervor of love for Me that you have for Me. The children are your responsibilities and these souls need to be brought to Me in the sacraments."**

I could see some large iron girders placed together as a new building was being constructed. Jesus said: **"My people, building your faith is like erecting a building. You first have to count the cost in that you are willing to give your whole will over to Me. Then you need a strong foundation so the building will stand up to the buffets of the weather. Lay your own foundation of faith on following My Commandments and those of My Church.**

The sacraments are your building blocks of faith as you go through life. Each one is timed for your place in life. When you have completed the work, your crowning touch will be when I receive you in Heaven."

I could see a tall building and the Antichrist sitting on a throne. Jesus said: "My people, your faith in Me will be tested dearly during the tribulation. The Antichrist will declare himself as Me and through lies and deceit, he will claim miracles of all that is good. He will say he is worthy of your homage, but do not follow him or worship him, even if you must die to refuse him. This evil one will be dispatched from his throne not long after he assumes full power over all the earth. My triumph will bring him to utter defeat and all of these evil ones will be cast into Hell. Rejoice, for My victory is not far off. Then you will enjoy the glory of My Era of Peace."

I could see a web of thorns. Jesus said: "My people, beware of this communication web that Satan has spun to ensnare many unsuspecting victims. Many of your technologies appear to have a good appearance, but they quickly are abused by evil men. This is another means to control your money and your buying and selling. This will become an instrument of the Antichrist's control. Even with evil men's seeming power, I will dash all of these things to complete destruction. My great chastisement will bring all evil men low and My power will reign over everything. I will recreate and renew the earth where no evil will be present. My glory will reign no matter what all the evil ones will do."

I could see an eagle with an unusual new head on the body. Jesus said: "My people, I am showing you that your nation will not be ruled as you know it today. You will soon have new leadership that will be devoid of all of the freedoms you have now. It will be a police state run by a tyrant under the control of the Antichrist through the UN. The One World people will finally claim their prize of world domination. These evil men will be double-crossed by the Antichrist and killed. Then this evil man will assume full power. This reign will be brief as I will declare My victory over all evil. Be joyous for you know the outcome of this final battle. All of My faithful will then be rewarded with My love and peace both on earth and in Heaven."

**Friday, May 29, 1998:**

After Communion, I could look down on a house where some men were lowering a paralytic through the roof. Jesus said: **"My people, during My ministry on earth some had faith, while others were lacking in their commitment. This incident of the paralytic showed great faith both in the man seeking to be healed, and in those who carried him. They were so confident in this man's healing, that they performed a heroic act to overcome the crowds around Me. I tell you, the more faith that you have in My works, the greater grace I will bestow among My believers. So, believe in My miracles and you will see wonders performed before your very eyes. He who knocks on My door in faith, he will have his prayers answered to the fullest. Continue in your prayer requests, since you have seen many miracles performed even in your day. I love all of My people so much, and I will see to all of your needs when you ask in My Name. Be ever prayerful in your intentions, and by your deep faith, you will be healed in your physical and spiritual needs."**

Later, at St. Phillip Neri Church, Albuquerque, N.M., I could see some special wood carvings of statues and icons. Jesus said: **"My people, the roots of My Church are deep over the years here. My people here have been very faithful to My ways. Those, who are close to Me and follow My Will, will be greatly rewarded. You have felt a special presence of Mine here as you had a sense of shaking under your feet. This church is more than a tourist memory. It represents an endurance of the people's faith. I draw all of My people to Me through the pouring out of My love. Even though a trial will come upon the world, I will protect you and provide for you through your faith in My Name. Rejoice in sharing My presence among all of these faithful in this church."**

**Saturday, May 30, 1998:**

At St. Bernadette Church, Albuquerque, N.M., after Communion I could see a large cross on the altar and then many smaller crosses all around it. Jesus said: **"My people, I have asked you many times to pick up your cross and carry it with Me to Calvary. I had to suffer for your souls, so you must suffer in this** life as well. I ask you to always follow My Will, by letting you die to self. When your will gets in the way of My Will, I can not work through you. You must open your heart and have an open mind to discern My plan for your life. So I ask you, My friends, that whatever you do, that you do it for My glory only. If you should so something only for your own glory and pride, then you are not doing it for the right purpose. Let this be a test for what you are doing. If what you are doing is for My glory only, then continue in that work. But if what you do is only to make you look good, then you should refocus your energy on things for Me only. The evil one will distract you with things that make you feel good about yourself. Do not let your pride distract you with too many things of the world. I alone am your God, and I alone should you worship."

**Sunday, May 31, 1998:** (Pentecost Sunday)
At the Lord's Ranch, Vado, N.M., after Communion I could see a dove and then darkness with a small flickering flame. The Holy Spirit said: **"My children, I am the Spirit of Love and I come to share My infinite love with all of you. As you see this flame of My love over each of you, know that I instill My Spirit in all of you as well. It is this love of God and love of neighbor that I am asking all of you to follow. By giving your will over to Me, I can have My gifts blossom in your life. It is important to see in the readings how you need to keep an open mind without**

THE

LORD

the protection of your comfort zone. All of My messengers and evangelists are living and breathing My Spirit when you go where I send you. Do not be afraid to do uncomfortable things for Me and continue to witness the Gospel in public so souls can be saved. The thrust of your ministry to save souls from Hell with My help is an inspiration to all those ministering for My Church. Follow My Will and the direction of My Spirit and you will win your prize of being with Me in Heaven. Al-

ways remember to use your gifts for the Lord and remember that no matter how much you do, without love, it is nothing. Love is the core of life and I ask all of you to live your love of God and love of neighbor."

**Monday, June 1, 1998:** (St. Justin)

After Communion, I could see many people in a Church walking down the aisles to receive Holy Communion. In the next scene I could see the Church had been flattened and all the stones were evenly spread out. (Mark 13:1-2) Jesus said: **"My people, many of your physical churches will be thoroughly destroyed to the ground. You will see this persecution of My Church come to a height of evil where My Churches will be sought out by evil men. They will try to kill My faithful and some will be martyred, while others will escape into hiding. My faithful realize that they will have to have Masses in secret. But if there is not a priest available, pray for a spiritual communion. I have been giving many messages about the coming schism and a split in My Church, so you will be spiritually prepared. This is also a sign that this time of persecution draws closer. You will all be tested and each clergy and lay person will have to decide either to follow the Antipope or My Pope son John Paul II. This decision may seal the fate of how many will be judged. Those, who side with the Antichrist, will be condemned to Hell, while those, who side with Me, will be saved."**

Later, at Adoration, I could see some poor small houses out in the rural area. Jesus said: **"My people, I am showing you the simple life on the farms, that I will be drawing you to. You have grown apathetic with your riches, and too sophisticated with your technology. You do not need all of these things and they are becoming idols for you. You are depending more on yourselves than on Me. That is why for your own spiritual welfare, I will be stripping your possessions from you. When you come to Me in full trust of what I will provide for you, then you will be able to grow in your spiritual perfection. Have Me in full focus at all times, so you will not be distracted by worldly things. I love all of you, but each soul must be tested, so that you can choose to love Me of your own free will."**

**Tuesday, June 2, 1998:**

After Communion, I could see a lecture hall with tiered seats, but they were all empty. Jesus said: **"My people, you spend many years going to school and college and are very attentive to all of your teachers. Yet, you have the greatest of teachers in Me and few are willing to study the words I have revealed to you. Many have Bibles, but how many are read often? You take a considerable amount of time to study courses of your own choosing, but how many will give Me time in reading and understanding My Word? The subjects that you study may help you in worldly things, but these things do not have a lasting value. If you want to learn how to gain eternal life, you need to spend some of your valuable time reading My Words of life in how to imitate a holy life. You have very little time in this life relative to the time you are to spend in eternity. Do you not think it is wise to study about how you are to reach your desired destination? Reflect on My Word and you will be prepared to be with Me in Heaven."**

Later, at Adoration, I could see a circular castle tower. This was followed by a common house. Jesus said: **"My people, this is a sign to you that a well-known leader will be stepping down from his position. This will begin a series of leaders losing their jobs as the Antichrist and his agents will start to assume power. Many will be uneasy during a chaotic disruption of order. Financial and political turmoil will provide the environment for this so-called man of peace to take over the heads of government. There will be a New World Order brought about by the One World people and this Antichrist will be their new leader of the whole world. This man will have miraculous powers and you will need to avoid his influence. He will demand worship from every one, but his reign will be brief. Just when these evil men will cheer their victory, I will lay them low as my power will overcome them. They will suffer in hell as I renew the earth with no evil present. Your joy then will know no end."**

**Wednesday, June 3, 1998:**

After Communion, I could see a very strong storm at night with lightening and telephone lines down. Jesus said: **"My people, you have seen many high winds and tornadoes in various places** in your country. You are being tested with these chastisements to bring you to your knees in prayer. When you have your possessions stripped from you, you can see how they do not last long on this earth. But you are an immortal spirit that will last into eternity. You are taken up with your possessions, but you cannot take them with you past the grave. That is why I am showing you how these things are of little importance to you at the judgment. These things can distract you from praying to Me and giving Me glory for all of this Creation. Only spiritual things are of everlasting value, and how you live your life for Me, is how you will be judged. So, see these storms as a wake-up call to show your vulnerability in this life. If you were to be killed today in such a storm, would you have your life in order to come to Heaven? If you are not ready, then come to Me in Confession for the forgiveness of your sins. See that this life is only a testing of your love for Me. Only those, that love Me and accept My ways, can enter into Heaven. Your eternal destination of your soul is the most important concern of your life."

## Thursday, June 4, 1998:

After Communion, I could see a large rock in a cave with the Ten Commandments inscribed in it. Then there was someone kneeling and praying at the light of the entrance to a cave. Jesus said: "My people, no matter what you may face in life and during the tribulation, do not lose sight of your obvious commitment to love of God and love of neighbor. These are the basis for My Ten Commandments and they should be the model by which all society should live. Do not let your own selfishness nor the ways of the world turn you away from following My Commands. Every sin and the punishment due for that sin must be made up for in forgiveness and suffering in order for you to enter into Heaven. Do not let Satan or your peers deceive you in their lies, so that you think acts against My Commandments are not sins. Evil exists and the demon angels exist as real spirits. When you do things that offend Me, remember My forgiveness awaits you as the love of the prodigal son's father. Do not fear confessing your sins, but look upon this sacrament as a way to restore our bond of love and keeping you on track to Heaven. If you sin against My Commandments and have no sorrow for your offenses, you are leading yourself to eternal punishment in Hell. I love all of My souls with an unending love, but My justice must prevail along with My mercy. Seek My mercy every day and you will not be far from the reign of God."

Later, at the prayer group, I could see some American Indians sitting in front of some pictures with a fire burning. Jesus said: "My people, I ask you to pray for all of the American Indians whose land was taken as you spread westward. Many injustices were suffered by these native peoples. Fighting for land in your country has a history which many have forgotten. These people were displaced from their homes by your settlers. History will soon repeat itself, only this time it will be the evil Antichrist who will take possession of your homes."

I could see a scene in the desert and a gleaming city came forward with many pyramid shapes. Jesus said: "My people, a New World Order will rise up in your midst at the hands of the Masons. They will quickly take control of all of your countries. This plan has been in planning awaiting the time of the Antichrist. I told you many signs in the skies will indicate the coming of this evil age. Evil may reign for a time, but My victory is assured. Keep faith in Me no matter how severely you will be tested."

I could see a large structure to represent the image of the beast. This became a shrine that everyone was forced to worship. Jesus said: "My people, idolatry and blasphemy will reach its height when the evil Antichrist will try to force everyone to worship his image. His agents will go from house to house enforcing his edict to worship him and take his mark in the hand. Without such a mark, one could not buy and sell. This will be the height of your evil age. But at its height I will send My justice as a comet to destroy and defeat the Antichrist and all of his armies. My power will reign supreme and all the evil ones will gnash their teeth as they are all cast into Hell. Endure this trial but a moment and then you will enjoy My triumph in a new land."

I could see many massive fires and huge thunder heads of storms that will test the people. Jesus said: "My people, you will suffer many hardships in the coming fires and storms. These storms will increase in their frequency and intensity. My chastisements will reach even to those areas thought safe from this destruction. Your weather changes are a sign to you of how I am displeased with your sins and your indifference to seek My forgiveness of your sins. As you are all brought to your knees in testing, prepare spiritually to have your soul in readiness for My coming."

I could see a golden glow over the land and a beautiful blue sky. Jesus said: **"My people, those, who are faithful to Me through this tribulation, will live with Me in this coming Era of Peace. All of those present will wonder in awe at the beauty of My re-creation of the earth. Everything will be provided for you and you will marvel at your new garden of paradise. You will give praise and glory to Me every day as the angels. You will continually thank Me for living in this new world of My peace with no evil present."**

There was a bright orange light as a large sunset with a stairway to Heaven. Jesus said: **"My people, as the age of My Era of Peace comes to a close, all of you will reach perfection enough to be allowed into Heaven. I will be preparing you for Heaven while you perfect yourselves in My Age of Peace. My holy ones will teach you all that you need to know to reach your perfection in Heaven. These teachers will be those that I will raise up from their martyrdom for My Name's sake. Rejoice as you are graduated from this earthly heaven up to My glorious Heaven. This will be a reward to My faithful beyond your dreams."**

I could see a large dove flying with a branch of peace. The Holy Spirit said: **"My children, I am the Spirit of Love and I come to share My graces of your Pentecost. Pray, My children, for peace in your world. You have seen this image of peace many times, but it is up to you in your hearts if peace will reign. If there is not enough prayer for peace, you could see some nations annihilated in nuclear war. You are always battling the evil one with the grace I give you. Stay strong in your prayer commitment and you will go with less stripes against you."**

**Friday, June 5, 1998:**

After Communion, I could see about ten pens grouped together. Jesus said: **"My people, I am showing you many pens, because I** used many instruments in writing down the words of Scripture. They were inspired by the Holy Spirit to reveal the truths of My life and My teachings. Just as I revealed My truths during the Old Testament and after My death to St. Luke and St. Paul, I allow prophets in every age. Even, today, you are blessed with many visionaries who are given words to lead you to Me. I have told you also that you will see many false prophets in the end days to confuse My faithful. Again, test the spirit of every prophet by their allegiance to Me and if their words are in accord with Scripture. I do not leave you orphans. That is why I am sending My prophets in every age to teach you and make you aware of My ways. My words of love go out to you in every age. You are blessed to remain open to My Word."

### Saturday, June 6, 1998:

At Our Lady of Grace, Minneapolis, Minn., after Communion, I could see a large cross with a corpus on the altar at Mass. Jesus said: **"My people, look upon My Cross as a sign of My love. Keep My Cross and Corpus before you in the church, on your person, and on the walls of your homes. When I died for all of you on the Cross, this was My most perfect act of My love for you. By shedding My blood for you I became the sacrificial lamb for you. It is by My gift for you that all mankind has been ransomed. Now, the Gates of Heaven are open for you and by your acceptance of Me as your Savior, you are welcome in faith to come to Me in Heaven. Seek the forgiveness of your sins which I have gained for you. Everything I do is for you. I ask only that you follow My Will and do everything for Me. When you go through life, remember that everything you do and accomplish are done with My gifts and My grace. I say this so that you always give Me the credit for all that you do and have. In doing so, you will not be puffed up with your own pride. Give glory to Me for all that I do in creation and your life. Your crown will await you in Heaven as you fight the good race and finish this life. By suffering each day with Me and consecrating your every action to Me, I will walk with you and give you the grace to sustain you in your daily trials. When you look on My Cross, see this as a symbol of My victory over sin and death and not a sign of defeat. This is your**

E-mail

Find John Leary

http://www.frontiernet/

net ~ vyyperl

symbol also that you must suffer in life with your own cross, so you can gain eternal life by your own Calvary."

Later, at Holy Family Adoration, Minneapolis, Minn., I could see a large brilliant light at night and it appeared to be the light by which our guardian angel will lead us in the tribulation time. I asked Jesus for permission of Mark to speak and he said: **"I am Mark and I stand before God. Many have wondered how their angels will lead them to hiding in the time of the tribulation. There will be a physical light as in the Exodus to show you the way to a safe haven or a cave. The Lord has told you to have full trust in His Word that you will be led to a safe place. It is not necessary to make any financial preparations, but to have faith that you will be led to safety. Do not worry about the uncertainty of your destination in the world since we will be protecting your souls. Some will be martyred in this time and others will be fully protected at holy ground places or in the caves. Pray for courage and the power of the Holy Spirit for what to do and where you are going. Have no fear, because Jesus will watch out for His faithful ones. Follow your angels by their signs to you and you will find your destination. As long as you are faithful to God in your heart, you will live to see Jesus in the glory of His Era of Peace. Thank Jesus for all He is doing for you in this life."**

### Sunday, June 7, 1998: (Holy Trinity Sunday)

At Our Lady of Grace, Minneapolis, Minn. after Communion I could see a home with a wife, a husband, and the children. Jesus said: **"My people, I am showing you a sign of human love that you experience among your family members. This is a unity of people that is united with Me through the Sacrament of Marriage. Think of the Trinity as Spiritual Persons united by an infinite love. The Father generates the Son and our love generates the Holy Spirit which is love personified. We are joined as Three Persons in One God. I have told you in the Scriptures that I did nothing without doing it with the Father. I have said many times how the Father and I are One in the Spirit. Just as I have called two in marriage to be of one flesh, the Three Persons of Us are joined in One Spirit. Each person of a marriage** is separate, but each of Our Persons are known by Ourselves. Just as each member of your families perform different tasks, each of Our Persons are called to different functions as you understand them. Our Trinity is a mystery of faith, but know that love is the core bonding force. Our love extends out into all of creation so We can share Our love with all of you. Rejoice and be glad for all that We do for all of creation."

**Monday, June 8, 1998:**

After Communion, I could see holes in the floor of a Church and then a scene of a Church stripped of all the statues, altars and pews. Jesus said: **"My people, I have told you how you will be stripped of your possessions in the worldly things by storms and fires. This testing is to wake you up to test your faith in Me. Those, who rely on these things, will be saddened to lose them, but it will be better for your soul. The next test will be the evil people, who will be secretly undermining your churches. They will gradually strip your churches of kneelers, statues and crosses all in the name of renewal and modernism. Even My tabernacles are being hidden in rooms away from the main body of the church so that it will be hard to find. Why are you allowing these evil people to remove the traditions of your past? These churches will become so devoid of anything holy that they will become just a shell of a building. Preserve the statues and crucifixes for your underground Masses. As religious persecution will increase, you will have to hold your Masses in secret. Eventually, you will have to go into hiding away from the Antichrist's agents who will try to kill you. You may suffer for a while, but I will soon condemn this evil lot to Hell in My triumph over evil. I will restore the beauty of My original creation, so My faithful will enjoy a bliss of following My Will with no obstructions. Pray and remain faithful and you will enjoy your reward in My Era of Peace and in Heaven."**

Later, at Adoration, I could see two people looking forward at a TV, and they were like robots the way they were being controlled. Jesus said: **"My people, I am showing you the spell that those, who take the Mark of the Beast, will be under. When people sell their souls to the Antichrist, by worshiping him and taking** his mark, they will be among the living dead. The Antichrist will then control your mind and he will have you seek out My faithful to kill them. Those with the mark will be your persecutors and you should flee from them as much as the Antichrist and his agents. Even if you should know these people, they will not spare you any mercy. Once people have given themselves over to the evil one, they will have little control over their actions. These people will be condemned to Hell, because they worshiped the prince of evil. That is why it is paramount that you have the people not take this chip in the hand or they will be lost. My mercy will be on those who are forced against their will to take this chip. But My justice will fall on those who willingly submit to the Antichrist and give him full allegiance. No matter what the Antichrist will offer you to go with him, refuse his lies and his enticements. You should rather be martyred than worship anyone else but Me. Pray for all men when they will be forced to make this decision between Me or the evil one. I will provide for you in both your physical and spiritual needs. Never leave Me or you will face an eternity in Hell. I love all of My souls and I will give you the grace to endure this test to show your love for Me."

Tuesday, June 9, 1998: (Elijah, woman, cakes)

After Communion, I could see a line of sacks of flour standing vertically. Jesus said: **"My people, you must have hope and trust in My Words when I promise to provide for My faithful during the tribulation. I have shown you in the readings how I provided for My prophets. Even though many of My prophets have been killed and persecuted, I ask them to go out and declare My prophetic words in public. For those that are called to go forth, do not be reluctant or afraid to declare a hard message. Instead, speak the truth of what is to come and how the people should read and follow My Words. When the tribulation comes, believe that I will feed you My Heavenly Manna. I will multiply your food for all to see, so that you will not be tempted with the food of the Antichrist. These lessons in the Scripture, concerning the multiplication of food, are an inspiration to you that I will continue to provide for you. My grace and gifts are** available to all that need them. So call on My help at any time and I will listen to your prayer."

Later, at Adoration, I could see some large ads on billboards advertising the advantages of the Smart Card. Jesus said: "**My people, you will be experiencing a massive campaign to try and have everyone switch to a smart card for all of your transactions. Electronic transactions will be encouraged even over cash and checks to show you how easy and safe these new cards can be. Every means of persuasion even to subliminal ads on television will be used to get you used to smart cards for all of your money dealings. They will show you how one card will do everything and it will reconcile your records easily and help at tax time. Every excuse will be used to gradually force smart cards as the only means of exchange. I have told you that these chips will be the forerunner of the same chip in the hand or forehead. You will not be condemned for using the smart card, but I am encouraging you to refuse this card, because it will then only be obtained in the hand or forehead. They will tell you how it is better for security, but do not be fooled into using it. Know that when they try to force these chips on everyone, it will be the time to go into hiding. For the next step will be to force you to take the chip in the hand or they will persecute you in the detention centers. The Antichrist will appear to gain control for a brief time, and then I will bring My triumphant hand of justice against him and remove him from the earth into Hell. Follow these events on the smart card and avoid the Antichrist's control before it starts by not taking the chip at all.**"

### Wednesday, June 10, 1998:

After Communion, I could see a hole going down into the ground. Then I saw some liquid come up out of the ground in a stream. Jesus said: "**My people, I am showing you how the molten magma comes up out of the ground in a volcano. There are many active sites all over the world, but only a few send large amounts of ash into the air. Smoke from fires and volcanoes can blot out the light of the sun causing it to grow darker. Droughts will continue to cause more fires and earthquakes will trigger more volcanic action. You will see more and more pollution caus-**

ing breathing problems in some areas. As more of these natural disasters come, people will become more uneasy and your life, as you know it, will be more chaotic. It will be a time when you see financial and political disturbances that the Antichrist will appear as a man of peace to solve your problems. Do not follow him, but only worship Me and give allegiance to My Commands. After the test of evil, I will calm everything and you will experience peace and love in My new Era of Peace."

**Thursday, June 11, 1998:** (St. Barnabas)

After Communion, I could see some people in a building and they were worshiping a large golden pyramid as a god. Jesus said: "My people, there are worldly people that will lie, kill, and steal for wealth and power. These are the same people who will worship these alien symbols of power as the golden pyramid. For some, this is their new golden calf of the lost generation of Israel. Wealth can become an obsession without any real purpose. Once you have wealth beyond your physical needs, there is only pride drawing people to have more prestige for what they can buy. This burning desire to have more money drives people to search in unlawful means to acquire it. For this reason money can be the root of most evil. So listen to the words of the readings when I sent My Apostles out with no money to preach the Gospel. My faithful do not need to pursue wealth since the worldly have this as their goal. Seek to please Me first and I will provide for all of your needs. Many of the rich have sad faces because once they have followed Satan's call to riches, there is an empty feeling because the spirit is not satisfied with earthly things. Those of less means, that have a richness in faith, are truly happy in My grace, for their souls are satisfied in the peace I bring to their spirits. True happiness can only be found in Me and not money. The pleasure of wealth is fleeting, while spiritual richness in Me gives eternal joy."

Later, at the prayer group, I could see two large murals of saints on the walls of a cave. Jesus said: "My people, I have asked you to preserve your statues and icons of Myself and the saints. In doing so, you can call on the help of the saints and Myself in your daily trials. As more of you are persecuted, you will be hiding in the caves or holy ground safe havens. Rejoice, that I will be with you throughout the tribulation."

I could see a stairway leading up to a chapel of perpetual adoration. Jesus said: "**My people, you are blessed to have an increasing number of perpetual adoration chapels. These are channels of My grace for all who wish to partake of My Adoration. Do not worry about time, but drink in My Spirit so your heart can be renewed with My blessings. I am calling out to many souls to come and visit Me in all of My glory. Those who do not come to see Me, are missing out on many graces and a deeper peace in My love.**"

I could see some yellow gleaming walls of the new Jerusalem. Jesus said: "**My people, I have told you that I will create a new Jerusalem that I will bring down to earth. It will be made of many rare stones and its walls will gleam with My light. Those, that live in the Era of Peace, will be spiritually fulfilled to see My peace and love on earth without any evil. You will all be witnesses of My splendor as you grow in perfection.**"

I could see some cheerful faces as they were giving glory and thanks to Jesus. Jesus said: "**My people, look with eager anticipation for when My faithful will live in My new Era of Peace. You will have perfect temperatures at all times. Vegetation will be all about you and it will replenish by itself. You will enjoy the beauty of creation with a full knowledge and understanding of how life works. You will all live long lives because you will have the advantage of My Garden of Eden with all of its life giving elements. Have hope and trust in your testing time and this joy of a perfect world will be yours to share.**"

I could see some temples with a strange yellow light during the night. Jesus said: "**My people, this is another scene of the Era of Peace where you will experience temples of light and places to worship Me at any time of day or night. You will have no fear of any war again. Even your fear of animals will be removed as you can caress any of them without any bites or stings. The harmony of this world will so overwhelm you, to see how everything can be without the effect of evil.**"

I could see Mary with her heart exposed along side of Jesus with His heart open as well. Mary said: "**My dear children, this is** the month of Our Two Hearts and many have joined in this beautiful devotion. Our Hearts are one and they are open to all of you to share every day. Call on each of Us to give you the grace to endure this age. I lead you to my Son and I offer up all of your petitions to Him for you. My Son listens to your every plea and He answers you in the best way for your soul's benefit."

I could see some various forms of charts both on paper and on a computer. Jesus said: "My people, you are always charting everything that changes in your world. It would be an interesting chart if you could chart your spiritual progress in life. If you truly loved Me, you would work very hard to improve by your works and prayers each day. To advance in your spirituality, you need to note somehow where you are and what you have improved. You may have some failures, but be able to pick yourself up and learn from your mistakes. By always checking to see if you are gaining or losing, you can see where you need improvement. Ask My help and the help of holy people around you for advice on how to better your lives. This is a lifetime job which you cannot stop trying to better yourself. Then when you meet me at Heaven's Gate, I can say enter in, My true, faithful servant."

### Friday, June 12, 1998:

After Communion, I could see some large blocks of a small Church opening up to a busy road. Jesus said: "My people, many times with the tensions of your busy days, it is like an oasis to come into a little church to visit Me. When you are tried by the trials of the day, it is refreshing for your spirit to come and seek My graces of help. You do not have to face your troubles alone. I am always eager to walk with you and give you that spiritual lift to see your way. If the stress of life has you down, do not reach for some headache medicine, but reach for your Rosary or prayer book. When you communicate your spirit to Me in prayer, I will settle your fears and tensions. Lay your problems on My shoulders and I will bear your burdens. By having faith in My answering your problems, you will wonder how you became upset over very little. Do not let life's little annoyances upset your peace. Let Me slow your life's pace down and you will be at ease once again. It is the evil one who tests you with anger. When you take time to put things in a spiritual perspective, worldly things are not so much to be concerned about. Seek My help first, and all of your needs will be provided for."

Later, before the Blessed Sacrament I could see the rear taillights of a car as the break lights went on. Jesus said: "My people, following My Commands is like following your traffic rules. When you are driving, you can see the immediate danger in going through red lights or stop signs. If someone is coming from the other direction, you can cause an accident with loss of life. But you have free will with either your gas pedal or your brake pedal to make the right decision. With sin it is only obvious you are wrong, if you love Me and still violate My Commandments. Your understanding of natural law indicates to you that it is not right to lie, kill or steal. Yet, again you have free will to exercise your decision. As you commit one sin, you become weak and you may continue sinning. It is only when you realize how sin offends Me and the guilt of your actions, that you may change your ways. I have given you the Sacrament of Reconciliation to have sorrow for your sins and seek your forgiveness. On earth the courtroom determines your sentence. In Heaven it will be My judgment that determines if you will be in Heaven or be eternally lost in Hell. Think first therefore, before you decide on your actions, and consider the consequences when you go against My laws."

### Saturday, June 13, 1998:

After Communion, I could see a butterfly. Jesus said: "My people, as you look on the stages of life in a butterfly, you see that it becomes a thing of beauty from a crawling worm. This is the metamorphosis that a new Christian must go through. You were in a life of sin, but now you must put away the desires of the world and think only of Me and Heavenly things. You must become like the grain of wheat. Unless the grain dies, it cannot sprout into a new ear of wheat. So it is with you in your soul. You have to die to self and now live in My Will by giving your will over to Me. Then one day my faithful will go through their own metamorphosis when you are resurrected with your glorified body and soul. When you are transformed into the real now, away from time, you will put on the white robes of faith and enjoy the glory of Heaven. I love all of you so much and I call all of you to this change in your lives. It is only by an act of your free will that you can die to self and live forever with Me."

Later, at St. John's Preparatory Adoration, Danvers, Mass. I could see some glass structures on some buildings being threatened by storms. (It was raining very hard on a skylight.) Jesus said: "**My people, as you witness the storms all around you, I am reminding you of My Word that I will test your country dearly with storms and fires. You will be brought to your knees not only to seek the forgiveness of your sins, but you will be petitioning Me to take these chastisements away. When your possessions are damaged and you are no longer comfortable, you will wake up to the fact that I alone am your Lord. On bended knees you will all recognize My Kingship and no other is deserving of your praise than Me. My faithful understand My glory, but even the disbelievers, I will get their attention. For some, it takes a severe thrashing to make them come to their senses. You are not sent here just to enjoy an easy life, but to pick up your cross and serve Me by following My Will. For those, who still fail to listen to My warnings, they will face an eternal suffering in Hell. I call everyone to love Me, even the most grievous of sinners. Harken to My cry and believe that I am your Savior. Your time is short and you need to make your life decision of either coming to Me in love or following the hate of Satan.**"

**Sunday, June 14, 1998:** (Corpus Christi)

At Sacred Heart Church, Ipswich, Mass., after Communion, I could see a large alpha and omega represented in Jesus. Jesus said: "**My people, I am the Alpha and Omega, the Beginning and the End. I am the living bread of life. He, who eats My Body and drinks My Blood, has eternal life in them and I will remain with you until the end of time. This is a hard saying to understand that My Real Presence of My Body and My Blood is truly present under the appearances of the bread and wine. When the priest properly consecrates the Host and wine, I will always be present for you. Remember after the first Mass on Holy Thursday that My one suffering of My life on the Cross ful-**

filled the promise made for all ages. My death is your ransom of your sins and Heaven's Gates are open once again. I ask only that you confess your sins in Confession, so your souls are ever pleasing to Me before receiving My Eucharist into your heart. Do not violate My gift of life with any sacrilegious Communions. I hold out My hand to draw you to My heart. My bread of life is your daily living bread which lasts forever. Receive Me in grace and I will fill your hearts with My joy and peace. Give thanks for the many gifts that I bestow on everyone. It is a blessing that you can receive My Real Presence. Honor and give reverence to My Blessed Sacrament wherever I am found. When you all are united in My one love, you have a share in My Mystical Body."

Later, at St. John's Preparatory Adoration, Danvers, Mass., I could see a beautiful parade of flowers going through the new Era of Peace with bright sunlight shining. Jesus said: "My people, when you look upon My Era of Peace, you will see a new creation. Many flowers and trees will constantly bloom and bear fruit. There will be such a beauty on earth, that it will seem as heaven on earth. The varieties and types of fruits and vegetables will be so plentiful, you will not even know of their previous existence. When I said I make everything new, it will include new plants and animals. You will have full knowledge of all of My creation, even to the last detail. Live now in faith so you can be one of My witnesses to the promise of My reward in the Era of Peace. Those, who pay the price of their crowns by their suffering in the tribulation, will be blessed for their troubles. No matter how much the evil ones will taunt you, be ever vigilant in your struggle to follow My Will only. Do not believe any of the Antichrist's lies or his illusions. They are all meant to distract you in the ways of the world. My faithful know better, because you know that I have created everything and all is under My power. So thank Me for this age that you are living in, and help prepare all of those souls around you to follow Me in all of your trials."

**Monday, June 15, 1998:**

After Communion, I could see people at Mass and the priest and servers were standing at the foot of the altar. In the next scene the priest was standing before a huge rocky cliff and the Church was gone. Jesus said: **"My people, today you are comfortable in your churches, but tomorrow they will be taken away by the Antipope. When My Pope son, John Paul II, is removed from his office, the Antipope will dominate and control the property of all of the Roman Catholic Churches. The priests and the laity will have to decide whether to go with the evil pope or split to be with the faithful remnant and hold underground Masses. My faithful will have to leave their comfortable churches because they will become corrupted with false teachings. You are being forewarned that the Antipope will worship the Antichrist and violate all of the teachings of My Apostles. You will be able to tell he is evil, when he changes the laws and rules of My Church. You are seeing the cliffs of some hills because not long after this split in My Church, you will have to flee for your lives. As the persecution of religion worsens by the Antichrist's agents, you will have to have your Masses out in the wilderness or in caves for secrecy. Have faith that I will remain with you even in spiritual communion for those who ask. Seek your guidance in My help and that of your guardian angels and you will be cared for even during this tribulation."**

Later, I could see a row of trees on the edge of a cliff. The cliff looked like a man-made gouge of the earth in a neat carving for a road. Jesus said: **"My people, mankind has scarred the earth and now nature is rebelling against man. You have used the land for your homes and cities. You pollute the air with your technology and now your comforts are causing your downfall. You are burning your rainforests and polluting your water. All of your abuses of the earth are beginning to be the source of your storms and the cause of your fires from scorching droughts. Everything on the earth has been touched by man where much of the natural balance has been disturbed. Your greed for wealth and possessions have led you to a confrontation with My creation. You should not be surprised then that because of your sins and your abuses of the earth, you are receiving many chastisements through your weather and earthquakes. Even your dabbling in life's building blocks has set many new diseases in motion to cause pestilence all over your world. You are seeing all of the signs of the end** times and many of them are coming about from your own hands. For this reason I will intervene supernaturally to remove all evil and re-create the earth to its original beauty. Rejoice, for what you are about to see will be marvelous to behold."

**Tuesday, June 16, 1998:**

After Communion, I could view things from the level of people's feet. Jesus said: "My people, just as in the readings, your sins can bring you low as a punishment. When you have a sense of your guilt, you too, should chastise yourself and confess your sins. No matter what social position you find yourselves, you are all equal in My sight and liable to judgment. Without the forgiveness of your sins, your punishment could be worse. As I spared the king of an embarrassing death for his punishment, you too can have less stripes by humbling yourselves in public and seeking My forgiveness. But he, who continues to sin against Me without contrition, will face a heavy judgment. You are all weak in this life. So do not get puffed up with pride that you are better than anyone else, since one day you may be brought low in your sins and you will be required to pay for your crimes. This life is a constant test of your will, but you need to keep confessing your sins so you may be cleansed in My sight."

Later, at Adoration, I could see an animal digging a home in the dirt. Jesus said: "My people, take a lesson from the animals in that you could dig out a home in the dirt of a hill as well. When the persecution comes, I have asked you to go into hiding away from your persecutors. Of the things I have asked you to take, there was a small shovel for such digging. If the hills you are sent to are all rock, I will have My angels carve out a cave for you. If there is enough ground for digging, you could make your own home where no one could find you. You will be surprised how industrious you can become, to save your life and possibly those of your family as well. I will protect My faithful in many ways and I will feed you in your need. Never fear that I will not help you. Even when your situation looks hopeless, I will defeat the evil ones in all of their attempts to steal your souls. Have faith and trust in My help and you will have everything provided."

**Wednesday, June 17, 1998:**

After Communion, I could see a sword that was resting behind a chair. Jesus said: "**My people, put away the sword of conflict and instead put on the gifts of the Spirit. It is time to love one another and not to take up arms against each other. Reach out with love from each of your hearts to everyone, even your persecutors. By uniting in love with each other, you will draw together all of the parts of My Mystical Body. By sharing My Sacramental Presence with each of you, you can bring My Real Presence to everyone you greet. Remember that without love, everything you do is in vain. For when you do things out of love, you do it for Me and not just for yourselves. Rejoice in My love even now on this earth as a preview of My coming love to be witnessed more perfectly in My Era of Peace. Encourage one another by showing your love for God and neighbor in all that you do.**"

**Thursday, June 18, 1998:**

After Communion, I could see a small puddle of purified silver. Jesus said: "**My people, I am showing you in this vision how each of you are placed on earth to be tried and refined in the spirit until you are purified to enter Heaven. I call on each of you to be perfect as My Heavenly Father is perfect. I realize in your weak human condition that you cannot achieve this on your own, but with My help, anything is possible. Ultimately, you are in a battle with good and evil to control your will. I have given you each a free will to choose to love Me or not, since I do not force My love on anyone. It is this dying to self so you can live in the Divine Will, that is your heavenly objective. Because you are a sinner by Adam's sin, you may fall at times seeking earthly things before Me. I have redeemed you on the cross from your sins, so all you need do, is seek My forgiveness and I will wipe your souls clean. You are cleansed and purified in Confession. Over time, if you learn from your mistakes, you will realize that My ways are better than your ways. It is a lifetime work to realize that I am calling all souls to be with Me in Heaven. Your souls are like silver that gets tarnished from the sulfur in the air and needs to be re-polished. Sin works the same way in making you unpleasing to Me. If you are to reach** heaven, you must be frequently cleansing your souls by seeking forgiveness in Confession. Even more, you should refine the purity of your love for Me by improving your spirituality in your prayer life. The closer you draw yourself to Me, the less you will sin and offend Me out of love for Me."

Later, at the prayer group, I could see a picture of the sun and it was blocked so I could see the corona. Jesus said: "**My people, you will continue to see signs coming from your sun that will signal the coming End Times. Many are becoming impatient about when these events will begin. You will see many signs before the Antichrist comes. These things will happen in My time and according to My Will and no sooner. Once the tribulation comes into being, you will be grateful that I have postponed this time.**"

I could see the stripes of our flag come into view. Jesus said: "**My people, your flag and I were united in the beginning of your country. Today, the vision of your flag is vague because many have taken Me out of their lives and have replaced Me with the idols of the world. When you lose your sense of the sacred in My Blessed Sacrament, how can you begin to know Me? Your country needs to praise and worship Me instead of raising false gods before Me. In all of biblical history you will find those, that worshiped other gods, were brought to utter ruin.**"

I could see some children brought to a baseball game even on Sunday. Jesus said: "**My people, look at where most of your crowds are found. There are more coming to your sports arenas than are coming to church. When you show your children that sports heroes are more important than the saints, you are teaching them that the world is more important than your afterlife. Nothing in this world is more important than Me. What good is it if you gained all the fame and riches possible and you lost your soul in the process? Your soul and its destination should be your main focus in life. So seek those things that will bring your soul to heaven first. All other worldly pursuits are distractions of the devil.**"

I could see a parade of missiles and other military vehicles. Jesus said: "**My people, do not trust your safety in your military weapons. All that is man-made is transitory and will not last. I am the One you should place your trust in. You will never** have any winners in war, because war is only destructive and takes lives. Therefore, continue your prayers for peace and stop building up your war machines. These things only magnify the hate between nations and you place everyone's lives in jeopardy on your small planet."

Mary came and she was smiling. Mary said: "**My dear children, thank you for your many Rosaries and continue to storm heaven with your prayers. It is important to keep your prayer groups going, for I need as many prayer warriors as I can use. Thank you also for the display of these pictures and all of those who provide them. See how pictures and statues help you to remind yourselves of who are your real heroes and models to follow.**"

I could see some nuns dressed in white robes. Jesus said: "**My people, there are many cloistered orders who spend most of their time in prayer. Pray, My children, that more holy vocations may come forth, for your world needs these souls to balance the sin in your world. Even the laity can voice your prayers in unison with these nuns to pray for the conversion of sinners. You may never know the true value of prayer until you see the next life. Trust in My telling you that prayer is your best weapon to defeat Satan and the evil ones. If you doubt this statement, look at all the distractions and excuses the devil uses to stop you from your prayers. Satan also knows the real value of prayer and he will stop at nothing to discourage you from praying.**"

I could see some sound waves indicating a speech pattern. Jesus said: "**My people, you will see how your technology will use voice patterns to identify you. This fingerprint of sound is but another means that the Antichrist and the One World people will use for buying and selling in the electronic controls over you. Your speech also can be harmful by what you say of others. Do not lie or gossip about your neighbor in bringing them shame. Instead, speak only kind and generously of each other as you show your love for your neighbor.**"

**Friday, June 19, 1998:** (Sacred Heart of Jesus)
After Communion, I could see a small modest home and then a picture of Jesus coming where He showed His heart. Jesus said:

"My people, I am knocking on the door to every house, whether they be rich or poor. In doing so, I am asking the people there to welcome Me into their homes. It is My love that I wish to share with everyone right where you live. This is not a faith that remains at church. It is a love and faith which you should witness everywhere you go. Some welcome Me by placing statues and pictures of Me in all of the rooms of their houses. Others have enthroned Me in their homes by special prayers of the priest. The question I ask of everyone is: how are you going to answer Me when I come knocking on your door? Will you receive Me with open arms or will you say that you do not have time for Me? It is how you answer My Call that will determine the destination of your soul. At the judgment, I will separate the sheep from the goats. My sheep follow Me wherever I lead them and these will see My glory in Heaven. The goats are those who refuse to follow My Will and do only their own will. It is those, who deny Me and close the door to My love, that will be cast into the flames of everlasting Hell."

Later, at Adoration, I could see the barrels of some large guns and some planes and missiles. Jesus said: **"My people, many are currently critical of the ethnic attacks on innocent civilians. If you look closer, you will see this as nothing more than the flaunting of a leader's dictatorial power over his own country. Some leaders use weapons to establish broader control over their subjects. Other leaders extract heavy taxes or write fiat laws to show their power. The effect is the same when leaders lord their power over all aspects of your lives. Before you are critical of other country's leaders, look at the liberties that you are losing in your own country. Policy making at the higher levels of your government are only made by a few, and not by the wishes of your people. Many people are close to prisoners by their own inaction in giving away their freedoms to leaders who have assumed control by fiat laws. Pray, My children, for peace and justice in your world, where evil men control your lives more that you want to believe."**

**Saturday, June 20, 1998:** (Immaculate Heart of Mary)

After Communion, I could see Mary come and then I could see a picture that made a mockery of Mary. Mary said: **"My dear** children, I am grateful to those who pray my Rosary and know the importance of prayer in your lives. This makes up for many who do not pray at all. There are also some, even clergy, who mock my Rosary as old fashioned and they discourage people from saying the Rosary. Even worse, some make detestable cartoons of me with my Son. These offenses against my Immaculate Heart are very painful and I shed many tears for these souls that are on the road to hell. Many protestants have criticized my name, and do not give me any honor, even when it is mentioned in the Bible. So, see how my Son and I have to suffer many insults from man's misunderstanding and his outright rejection. I still love all souls, as does my Son, but it makes it difficult to see how the evil one has misled many into sin, and have turned their hearts cold to Us. You see, my faithful, why many need your prayers, and without your help, these souls could be lost forever. Reach out to save any soul who will listen to your example and encourage the children to say my Rosary."

Later, at Nocturnal Adoration, I could see a blue book being thrown out from a picture on to this country. Jesus said: "My people, what you are witnessing is a special condemnation of the sin of your country. When Moses cast the tablets of the Ten Commandments on the golden calf, it was to condemn the idol worship going on. So it is with you, America, this blue book represents God's law and it is being cast upon your idol worship of worldly things. Your life styles defy what I have shown you in My Holy Family. Those living together heterosexually or homosexually are living in mortal sin, and are on their way to hell, if they do not confess their sins. Many worship sexual pleasure, sports, and money before Me. Is there any wonder that you are being chastised for your many sins? Until your people acknowledge Me as your Savior, you will be condemned by your sins. So turn your hearts toward My love and you will be saved. If you refuse My love, you will face eternal death in Hell."

**Sunday, June 21, 1998:** (Father's Day)
After Communion, I could see the green vestments of a priest. Jesus said: "My people, today, many of you are celebrating father's day, but these are the fathers with a small 'f.' You have

been empowered to be partners in creation during reproduction. But the real creative act is when God the Father brings the soul into being in that first fertilized egg. Without the life giving Spirit present in all of you, you would be nothing but a heap of dust. That is why only One is your Father and He is in Heaven with a capital 'F.' For every day is God the Father's day and every day a new life and even more are created. There are also deaths every day coming back to God the Father. So life is a never ending cycle of birth and death, until time will be no more. Give glory and thanks to God the Father for all that He does in Creation. It is His gift of life that you share in every day of your life."

Later, at Adoration, I could see an old bronze metal antique. Jesus said: "My people, things of this world have a different value to everyone. Many collectors value something old by its rarity, but it may be too unsightly for others. Spiritual things, as adoration of My Blessed Sacrament, again are valued differently based on people's faith and their love for Me. I have told you how I look into your hearts for the intentions of what you do. If you truly wish to seek Heaven, you know that it is important to give your will over to Me. The riches of eternal life far surpasses anything of worldly value. So keep your focus on the heavenly riches which will last forever. Those, who choose Me over the world, will be rewarded for choosing the better portion. Life is short, so value everything by how valuable I would find it."

**Monday, June 22, 1998:** (St. John Fisher)

After Communion, I could see some old pews in a small dark Church. Jesus said: "**My people, you have seen many struggles in My Church where authority has been contested. There have been many splits in My Church and you had to endure many evil men who wished to lord it over you. Religious persecution has been on going because man could never accept My authority. There have been martyrs for My Name in days gone by, as there are martyrs even in your own day. As the tribulation draws near, you will experience another split in My Church. You will be in a battle of good and evil fighting to save souls. As the time of the Antichrist comes, you will need My help to endure an** evil that you have yet to see. **Pray for spiritual strength, since you will be tested to the limit of your endurance."**

Later, at Adoration, I could see some green trees and then many African children playing. Jesus said: **"My people, you all are responsible for the spiritual and physical well-being of the children of the world. In addition to prayer and donations, you need to give of your time to help the children in every way that you can. You can help work toward the stoppage of abortion so the children may even have life. You can also work to teach the children both spiritually and those useful things of the world. You know how much I love the little children, when I called them to Me. Defend these little ones from drugs and abuse and protect them in every way that they need your help. When you do all of this for love of Me, you will receive many blessings. But if you neglect the children or abuse them in any way, you will have to answer to My justice. Show your love for the children and care for them at all times."**

**Tuesday, June 23, 1998:**

After Communion, I could see some trees and billowing clouds of smoke from a fire. Jesus said: **"My people, you are continuing to witness the drought and heat that are bringing your fires. Storms, droughts and fires will intensify during the next few months. Many of your conveniences and comforts will be endangered with this testing. People will become so upset with these problems, that you will be on your knees praying for rain. When the clouds do come, they are raining even more destruction. As your problems grow worse with time, you will begin to see the world famine take shape. As food supplies dwindle, no longer will people scoff at this possibility. The turmoil in your workplace will cause many financial disruptions and all of these events will lead up to the chaos of the tribulation. Once the Antichrist appears, your testing will just begin. Prepare, My children, as evil will have one last gasp. But soon My victory will vanquish evil and those faithful will receive My peace and harmony."**

Later, at Adoration, I could see a line of infantry marching in a battlefield with smoke all around. Jesus said: **"My people, you are looking down the road to war. Do not continue to make** weapons for war or you may come to a day when they will be used. Instead of threatening war with your neighbors, you need to do everything to seek peace among your nations. When you think more of loving your neighbor, there will be less reason to want war. Struggle further to be peacemakers among other hostile nations. Pray for peace that these weapons of mass destruction will not be used. Killing people in war is what Satan desires. Strive to fight Satan with your prayers for peace, so man will not lift a sword against his brother. You are all a part of My human family, so seek to love Me and your neighbor, and you can prevent wars from starting."

**Wednesday, June 24, 1998:** (St. John the Baptist)
After Communion, I could see some hot coals with some firebrands in the fire. Jesus said: **"My people, at your Baptism you are all branded to be Mine. Many of you were Baptized at birth or some days after. This is your initiation sign into being a Christian, when you were freed from the bonds of original sin from Adam. When you go to another's Baptism, you have the opportunity to repeat your Baptismal vows to acknowledge the beliefs of the creed. You also are doing a Rite of Exorcism in denying Satan in your life. This Sacrament of Baptism empowers all of My followers to be evangelists in bringing souls to Me. At the same time you receive this Sacrament, there is a call to repent of your sins. You may not have sins as a baby, but those baptized later in life see this time as a conversion experience. St. John Baptized those in the river so you can see this sacrament is a cleansing of sin from your souls. Rejoice that you have such beautiful role models to follow in both My life and that of St. John."**

**Thursday, June 25, 1998:**
After Communion, I could see some breastplates as in armor for a war. Jesus said: **"My people, you have just read about the Babylonian captivity and exile which is an example to all nations who refuse to follow My laws. Take note America of this past history or you will be forced to repeat it. I have been sending you many chastisements to bring you to your senses and change your immoral ways. If you refuse to take My advice**

EX LIBRIS i. д'АРК

about conversion, and you fail to repent of your sins, you will
have your country taken over and you all will be in exile as
prisoners. My judgment fell on the Israelites as they were exiled from their land. Time is running out for America as you
will be held fast against your will by foreign troops. Many do
not understand how quickly your freedoms could be taken away.
The One World people already are planning your captivity, and
it is only a matter of time before they will force you into prison
camps, if you do not worship the Antichrist. Prepare spiritu-

ally for this ultimate of chastisements and you will physically be led to places of refuge in hiding from the authorities."

Later, at the prayer group, I could see some cars in a line and the factory was closed. Jesus said: **"My people, for years you have struggled to gain good salaries in your factories. Now your greed for more has threatened your very jobs themselves. Your international companies are now seeking cheaper labor abroad and no longer do these employers care to keep these jobs only in America. So now your possessions will be stripped, as you will only have cheap paying jobs. Keep your focus on pleasing Me, instead of seeking the passing riches of this life."**

I could see a pack of long matches on sticks. Jesus said: **"My people, I am showing you the potential for fires when you experience the searing heat of a dry summer. Just as it is easy to strike a match for fire, these lightening storms can light such fires as well. The fires in Florida are just the beginning of your droughts. If your rain is taken away, you will see more potential elsewhere for fires. As your crops are further affected by your poor weather, signs of the coming famine will become more evident. It is not too late to start storing food for when none may be available."**

I could see some dried up river beds. Jesus said: **"My people, all over the world fresh water is being threatened. Salts are entering into more wells and the water table is lowering in some places. Deserts are claiming more soil from that available to grow crops. Water will be so precious, that desalinating the oceans may become economical. Be thankful wherever you have fresh water, for soon these supplies will be drying up. All of these trials are being given to test your faith. It is your chance to turn to Me and ask My help in your problems."**

I could see a tall tree and I also could see a major root structure to support that tree. Jesus said: **"My people, compare the needs of a tree with the spiritual needs of the soul. The tree needs water and nutrients which it must gain from a well developed root structure. Your souls also need to be deeply rooted in faith, so you can stand up to the winds of the world's desires. You need spiritual food to continue to cultivate your love for Me which you have in My Eucharist. Even when a tree is dam-**

aged, it makes natural repairs. For your souls your sickness in sin can be healed in forgiveness. Even as I talk of you as the branches and I am the vine, never be separated from Me or you will surely die."

I could see machinery making weapons and a large black cloud of smoke overshadowed it. Jesus said: "My people, why do you continue to make weapons to exploit money for a few rich people. It is the desire even of some evil men to cause wars for the purpose of making money from the production of armaments. This is the blood money that will bring a heavy price for these souls to suffer for their greed. Do everything to encourage love and stop the hate of wars. It is only the evil ones who seek destruction rather than peace and harmony."

I could see a log cabin out in the wilderness all set up to say Mass. Jesus said: "My people, many of My faithful are seeking to set up refuges out in the wilderness. As the tribulation comes, you also will seek safety away from the authorities. You will suffer much persecution for believing in My Name. Have patience and seek My help in full trust and your needs will be cared for."

I could see some unusual signs and logos to indicate evil symbols. Jesus said: "My people, beware of the many signs and symbols used by the occult and evil people. As evil gains more control over this world, these evil things will start to take on an evil power of their own. There will be channels through which evil will be directed. This is why it is so important to keep your Blessed Sacramentals around you and on your person. My Holy Cross with the Corpus, Holy Water and your Rosaries are very powerful in fighting off the influence of the demons. Since many demons will be released from Hell during the tribulation, it behooves you to seek My help, that of your guardian angels and these spiritual weapons. These will be your armor to fight the good fight for your souls."

### Friday, June 26, 1998:

After Communion, I could see a baptismal font with water in it. Jesus said: "My people, remember when you ask for a physical healing, that you must have a firm faith that you will be healed. It is not enough to heal the body, because you need to cleanse the soul first of your sins. Many times in My public healings I healed their sins first, or I declared because of their deep faith, I would heal them. Healing takes place in the spirit as well as in the body. Sometimes trials in sickness are a means for people to stop and reflect on their spiritual lives. Terminal patients have time to prepare for their impending judgment. So I continue to draw souls to Me and have them ask for My forgiveness of their sins. I seek My lost sheep from their birth until their dying day. Come forward and have all of your sins cleansed in your soul by your sorrow for your sins."

Later, at Adoration, I could see a lot of high tension wires on large stands. Jesus said: "My people, your electrical wires and stations are very vulnerable to stormy weather and sabotage when they stand in the open. You may see more brownouts and power outages as a result of the coming storms and hot droughts. You have learned to make yourself comfortable, but take away your power and many of your comforts become useless. When you are tested with the loss of your power and possessions, many will realize how unusual these events are. As you are tested, you will be brought to your knees seeking My help for your problems. If you relent of your sins and seek My forgiveness, My blessings could return. But if you continue in your sins, My blessings will be removed and you will suffer much. So choose Me now, before it is too late and you lose yourself to Satan."

### Saturday, June 27, 1998:

At Sacred Heart after Communion I could see a llama coming down the center aisle of Church. Jesus said: "My people, you are not animals, but spirit and body. So come appropriately dressed when you enter My house. Give Me honor and respect in your dress no matter how hot your weather is. When you come to a wedding, you dress to give respect to your hosts. When you come before your God, should I not receive even more respect? Do not dress immodestly, lest you cause someone to lust in looking on you. Be careful in everything you do, that it be proper to please Me by your actions. Show Me that you love Me by doing everything according to My Will. In doing this, you will be preparing yourself for Heaven."

Later, at Adoration, I could look down on a desk from very high up and it was all alone. Jesus said: **"My people, I am trying to show you that one person can have a huge effect on others around them. Think of how many people you come in contact with throughout the course of your lifetime. When you consider the battle for souls, each faithful person has many opportunities to give good example to others. Those, who are an inspiration in faith, give support to many people around them. You may only see a few of those you influence, but I see a larger picture where your influence for good could spread even wider than you can see. Think of all the souls to be saved that are walking around you. It is so important therefore that all of My children lead clean lives and give good example to those watching you. Seek My help to do all that you can to spread My Gospel message. By living My message every day, more souls will be drawn to Me. I send you many saints and prophets to lead you in following My Will. Imitate My models of faith and you will all not be far from Heaven. Give thanks to Me and My blessings for showing all souls how to love Me and find their way to Heaven."**

**Sunday, June 28, 1998:** (Fr. Jack's Retirement Mass)

After Communion, I could see a casket open with a large cross enshrined in it. Jesus said: **"My people, I have asked you to carry your cross your whole life long. Your only spiritual retirement will come as you pass to the grave. If you are fortunate in years to retire from your vocation, you will gain a reprieve of some stress. But even in your worldly retirement, you still are left to struggle with your cross. You may have a lighter load, but now you will be more responsible to have a good prayer life with your extra time. Your struggle against the evil one never ceases until your death. So keep praying to Me for help and follow My Will in all that you do. Make more of an effort to visit Me quietly and pray for the conversion of sinners. In retirement you now have more time to help your neighbor to come close to Me. I have told you before, that those, who are faithful throughout life's trials, will enjoy benefits you could only dream about."**

Later, at Adoration, I could see some closed doors where the Blessed Sacrament had to be stored for protection. Jesus said: **"My** people, for a while you will be able to worship Me openly in your churches and chapels. A time is coming when you will have to preserve My Real Presence in secrecy. So appreciate this special time you have left to openly adore Me and give Me thanks. Very few dedicated souls come to visit Me. I think by your complacency, you do not realize the treasure that you have in conversing with your God face to face. Pray to promote My adoration places, so that more people can share in the joy of witnessing My Real Presence. As your religious persecution grows worse, you may have to defend Me with your very lives. To die for My Name's sake will make you a martyr for My Eucharist. As My physical Hosts become scarce and hard to find, pray to Me for spiritual communion and I will have My angels bring My Host on your tongue. Give thanks that I will be present to you in My Eucharist until I come again."

**Monday, June 29, 1998:** (Sts. Peter and Paul)
After Communion, I could see a door to a prison being closed. Jesus said: **"My people, the faith of My early Apostles was strengthened by the Holy Spirit in what to say and do. Even despite the persecution of My Church, it continued to spread and multiply because I watched over it. I promised you that I would be with you to the end of time and that the gates of Hell would not prevail against My Church. Some may be martyred, but My models in the saints were enough to inspire many conversions. As these end days approach, there will be more martyrs for My Name's sake, but the evil ones will not eliminate My Church. Have faith in My works that I will triumph over the evil ones and they all will one day be chained in Hell."**

Later, at Adoration, I could see a wine bottle among some easy chairs. I then saw someone using drugs. Jesus said: **"My people, I am showing you how easy people can be led into substance abuse. Drinking starts out socially and gradually works into a dependency. Those with money again start out doing drugs because they can afford the habit, but soon their lives are a shambles. Those, who are weak and are looking for something to forget their troubles, find themselves in worse situations of bad habits. Drugs and drinking have ruined more lives because** they were looking for easy crutches instead of dealing with their problems. If these people reached out to Me for help, they would have found a spiritual joy which is better than any earthly high from drugs or drink. So reach out in prayer and physical help for these troubled abusers, so you can help them deal with their addictions. Do not give up on any soul, but keep struggling to bring them to Me, even in difficulty."

**Tuesday, June 30, 1998:**
After Communion, I could see a single eye looking in one direction and then in another. Jesus said: "**My people, you continue in your sins still oblivious to your modern day prophets. I have given many messages for people to repent and refrain from their sins, but still they do not want to listen. This is why I have told you to expect to be stripped of your possessions, for you are not changing your lives. In the readings it talked of how I warn the people of coming events through My prophets. Man has been warned repeatedly, but still they do not listen. That is why I am trying to get your attention with these many storms and fires. Man will eventually come to Me on his knees when He must accept the obvious, that all of this sin demands his forgiveness and punishment. In days past, the Israelites were chased from their homes for their transgressions. You too, America, will be tested for your lack of repentance for your many abortions and sins of the flesh. Pray now before you are forced to your knees.**"

(Mass of St. Irenaeus) After Communion, I could see some stained glass windows and pictures of some saints. Jesus said: "**My people, you are all grateful to share My one true faith with each other. You have been given a deep, rich heritage in the teachings of My Church and the models of the saints. Never doubt the gift of faith you have been given, but treasure it and share it with all you come in contact with. Give glory and praise to Me in how I have inspired great men and women with the Holy Spirit to stand up against heresies and defend My Church through all the ages. It is My faithful's responsibility to teach My Gospel to every one, and claim all of your gifts as coming from My power. Give credit to My grace for all that you accomplish spiritually, never letting your own pride get in the** way of your work. I love all of My people and I call all of you to be with Me on earth and in Heaven. Do all of your works of evangelism for love of Me. Let every act that you perform be a prayer to Me. In this way it will discourage you from doing anything sinful. Bring as many souls to Me as possible, because you are more responsible for having such a rich deposit of faith."

O MOST HOLY CONFESSOR OF THE LORD, BENEDICT, FATHER AND GUIDE OF MONKS, INTERCEDE FOR THE SALVATION OF US AND OF EVERYONE.

# Index

children
give responsible care (Jesus) 4/23/98
protect and help (Jesus) 6/22/98
responsibility for (Jesus) 5/19/98
take to Mass and Adoration (Jesus) 5/3/98
take to sacraments (Jesus) 5/28/98
chips
for buying and selling (Jesus) 5/23/98
choices
values in life (Jesus) 6/22/98
Church
a great celebration in (Jesus) 5/14/98
protected from gates of hell (Jesus) 6/29/98
Church and State
separation abused (Jesus) 4/7/98
Churches
destroyed (Jesus) 5/14/98
persecuted (Jesus) 6/1/98
strip statues, kneelers (Jesus) 6/8/98
worship will deteriorate (Jesus) 5/7/98
comet
defeat of Antichrist (Jesus) 6/4/98
will deliver triumph (Jesus) 5/14/98
Confession
confess sins (Jesus) 6/14/98
repent (Jesus) 5/20/98
restores bond of love (Jesus) 6/4/98
the grace to stay close (Jesus) 4/14/98
to reach heaven (Jesus) 6/18/98
conscience formation
on Church and laws (Jesus) 5/15/98
conversion
or be taken over (Jesus) 6/25/98
creation
confrontation with (Jesus) 6/15/98
reflection of His love (Jesus) 4/17/98
rejoice in power and love (Jesus) 4/13/98
sacredness of life (Jesus) 5/27/98
worship God, not earth (Jesus) 5/7/98
creatures of God
to know, love and serve God (Jesus) 5/7/98

cross
is a symbol of life (Jesus) 4/8/98
crosses
carry with Jesus (Jesus) 5/30/98
each one fits their cross (Jesus) 4/10/98
crown of thorns
to cleanse thoughts (Jesus) 5/21/98
crucifixes
gift of love (Jesus) 6/6/98
sign of suffering (Jesus) 5/28/98
cycle of life
life is very short (Jesus) 4/4/98
daily Mass people
special faithful (Jesus) 5/8/98
daily trials
seek His grace (Jesus) 6/12/98
dates
time directed by the Father (Jesus) 5/24/98
death
be always on guard (Jesus) 4/30/98
transition to life in Spirit (Jesus) 4/8/98
decisions
Pope vs. Antipope (Jesus) 6/1/98
detention centers
persecution in America (Jesus) 4/12/98
disciples
suffer persecution (Jesus) 5/12/98
diseases
caused by dabbling in cells (Jesus) 6/15/98
diseases & pestilence
of suspicious origin (Jesus) 4/14/98
diseases & plagues
cured at caves and refuges (Jesus) 5/4/98
Divine Mercy
receive Communion pure (Jesus) 4/16/98
Divine Will
assured of salvation (Jesus) 4/19/98
carry cross of life (Jesus) 4/27/98
carrying our crosses (Jesus) 4/10/98
die to self (Jesus) 6/18/98
die to self (Jesus) 5/30/98
perfection of the soul (Jesus) 5/17/98

dress
  wear respectable clothes (Jesus)   6/27/98
drugs and alcohol
  ruined lives (Jesus)   6/29/98
earthquakes
  increased by solar wind (Jesus)   5/16/98
Easter Sunday
  gates of heaven opened (Jesus)   4/12/98
Eastern Rite Churches
  pray for unity (Jesus)   5/16/98
economic changes
  jobs controlled (Jesus)   5/3/98
Egypt
  evil raised up from (Jesus)   5/14/98
electricity
  power outages (Jesus)   6/26/98
end times
  do not fear with God's help (Jesus)   5/24/98
  signs in the sun (Jesus)   6/18/98
enlightenment
  will see souls as God does (Jesus)   4/7/98
enthronement of Sacred Heart
  welcome in home (Jesus)   6/19/98
environment
  do not abuse resources (Jesus)   4/23/98
Era of Peace
  after brief suffering (Jesus)   5/12/98
  be faithful in tribulation (Jesus)   5/9/98
  full knowledge of things (Jesus)   6/11/98
  grow in perfection, no evil (Jesus)   6/11/98
  life giving elements (Jesus)   6/11/98
  love and peace (Jesus)   5/23/98
  new plants and animals (Jesus)   6/14/98
  no divisions (Jesus)   5/16/98
  prepare by being faithful (Jesus)   4/9/98
  re-creation of the earth (Jesus)   6/4/98
  teachers from martyred (Jesus)   6/4/98
  temples of light (Jesus)   6/11/98
Eucharist
  we become tabernacles (Jesus)   4/19/98
Euro coin, the
  symbol of monetary power (Jesus)   5/2/98

evangelization
  know, love & serve God (Jesus)   4/1/98
  St. Paul maintained (Jesus)   5/12/98
evangelize
  be a good example (Jesus)   6/27/98
  be prayerful and humble (Mother Cabrini)4/26/98
  save souls from hell (Holy Spirit)   5/31/98
  time is short, angels to help (Jesus)   4/2/98
  to bring lost souls to God (Jesus)   4/19/98
  value of each soul (Jesus)   4/3/98
evangelize (personal)
  avoid distractions (Jesus)   5/24/98
  love of God, or fear of hell (Jesus)   4/16/98
  many souls touched (Jesus)   4/22/98
  speak out in His Name (Jesus)   5/17/98
evil spirits
  Jesus will protect us from (Jesus)   5/1/98
  ready to devour us (Jesus)   5/11/98
Exodus
  we will suffer like them (Jesus)   4/12/98
faith
  lay strong foundation (Jesus)   5/28/98
  our true riches (Jesus)   6/11/98
faith, deposit of
  stand up to heresies (Jesus)   6/30/98
families
  seek love and unity (Jesus)   5/4/98
famine
  from storms and droughts (Jesus)   6/23/98
Father's Day
  with a capital F (Jesus)   6/21/98
Father, God the
  go through Jesus (Jesus)   4/30/98
  honor on Father's Day (Jesus)   6/21/98
fires
  in Florida, drought (Jesus)   6/25/98
  storms and droughts (Jesus)   6/23/98
fires and storms
  will increase (Jesus)   6/4/98
flag of United States
  united to God in beginning (Jesus)   6/18/98

**Prepare for the Great Tribulation and the Era of Peace**

| | |
|---|---|
| justice system | |
| not just (Jesus) | 5/7/98 |
| King of Universe | |
| willed all creation (Jesus) | 4/4/98 |
| leaders | |
| have a double standard (Jesus) | 5/14/98 |
| power and control (Jesus) | 6/19/98 |
| stepping down (Jesus) | 6/2/98 |
| life | |
| give praise and glory for (Jesus) | 5/27/98 |
| rebirth of new (St. Therese) | 5/7/98 |
| testing of our love (Jesus) | 6/3/98 |
| Light of Life | |
| puts love in hearts (Jesus) | 5/28/98 |
| living together | |
| mortal sin (Jesus) | 6/20/98 |
| Lord's Ranch, The | |
| feeds the poor (Holy Spirit) | 5/31/98 |
| love | |
| Jesus' heart burns for us (Jesus) | 4/8/98 |
| rejoice in His (Jesus) | 6/17/98 |
| the core of life (Holy Spirit) | 5/31/98 |
| Love of God | |
| suffers for our sins (Jesus) | 4/5/98 |
| manna | |
| provided by angels (Jesus) | 5/22/98 |
| mark beast, smart cards | |
| set up by one world people (Jesus) | 4/23/98 |
| mark of the beast | |
| do not take to buy and sell (Jesus) | 4/16/98 |
| outlaws if you refuse to take (Jesus) | 4/30/98 |
| under control of Antichrist (Jesus) | 6/8/98 |
| used to buy and sell (Jesus) | 6/4/98 |
| marriage bond | |
| do not violate (Jesus) | 4/30/98 |
| martyrdom | |
| do not be afraid (Jesus) | 4/20/98 |
| for those faithful not hiding (Jesus) | 4/2/98 |
| given grace to endure (Jesus) | 5/9/98 |
| Mary | |
| graces of the Holy Spirit (Mary) | 5/21/98 |
| intercedes for us (Mary) | 5/6/98 |
| thanks for rosaries, pictures (Mary) | 6/18/98 |
| masons | |
| control by one world people (Jesus) | 5/23/98 |
| One World Order (Jesus) | 6/4/98 |
| seek worldly power (Jesus) | 4/23/98 |
| work with the Antichrist (Jesus) | 5/22/98 |
| materialism | |
| we will be stripped of (Jesus) | 5/22/98 |
| Mercy Sunday | |
| love, mercy, graces given (Jesus) | 4/19/98 |
| messages | |
| convert many (Jesus) | 5/17/98 |
| not listened to (Jesus) | 5/6/98 |
| personal, time is short (Jesus) | 4/2/98 |
| miracle of Cana | |
| provide in tribulation (Jesus) | 5/21/98 |
| miracles | |
| performed today (Jesus) | 5/29/98 |
| miracles of the Eucharist | |
| truth of Real Presence (Jesus) | 4/5/98 |
| mockery | |
| of Blessed Mother (Mary) | 6/20/98 |
| money | |
| root of all evil (Jesus) | 6/11/98 |
| money and riches | |
| seek Kingdom of God first (Jesus) | 4/2/98 |
| moral decisions | |
| not on emotions (Jesus) | 5/15/98 |
| Mother Cabrini | |
| will help in mission (Mother Cabrini) | 4/26/98 |
| Mystical Body | |
| helped by service (Mary) | 5/28/98 |
| share in new life (Jesus) | 4/14/98 |
| together in love (Jesus) | 6/17/98 |
| natural balance of earth | |
| abused for greed (Jesus) | 6/15/98 |
| natural disasters | |
| to strip our possessions (Jesus) | 4/13/98 |
| New Age Movement | |
| worship of earthly gods (Jesus) | 5/7/98 |

prophets
 killed and persecuted (Jesus) — 6/9/98
 persecuted for word of reform (Jesus) — 4/28/98
 warn of events and to repent (Jesus) — 6/30/98
prophets & messengers
 instruments of the Word (Jesus) — 6/5/98
protection
 holy ground and caves (Jesus) — 6/6/98
 with faith in His Name (Jesus) — 5/29/98
protestants
 critical of Mary (Mary) — 6/20/98
Purgatory
 better to suffer on earth (Jesus) — 5/9/98
purified
 to enter heaven (Jesus) — 6/18/98
pyramid
 new golden calf (Jesus) — 6/11/98
re-created earth
 marvelous to behold (Jesus) — 6/15/98
Real Presence
 daily bread (Jesus) — 6/14/98
Redemption
 gates of heaven opened (Jesus) — 4/21/98
 Mary suffered in (Mary) — 4/7/98
 scripture fulfilled (Jesus) — 4/5/98
refuges
 set up for Mass (Jesus) — 6/25/98
religious persecution
 set up secret lists (Jesus) — 4/23/98
 some martyred (Jesus) — 6/28/98
remnant
 faithful no matter what (Jesus) — 4/15/98
repentance
 seek forgiveness (Jesus) — 5/7/98
Resurrection
 act of glory (God the Father) — 4/30/98
 conquered sin and death (Jesus) — 4/18/98
 gains chance of heaven (Jesus) — 4/16/98
 greatest miracle (God the Father) — 5/8/98
 new hope and new creation (Jesus) — 4/7/98
 prepare for your own death (Jesus) — 4/23/98
 this planet is graced (Jesus) — 4/13/98

Resurrection (Easter)
 victory over sin and evil (Jesus) — 4/11/98
retirement
 more time to pray (Jesus) — 6/28/98
Revelation, book of
 being fulfilled (Jesus) — 4/30/98
sacramentals
 for protection (Jesus) — 5/14/98
 guard for protection (Jesus) — 5/5/98
 have in each room (Jesus) — 4/28/98
 protect from evil spirits (Jesus) — 5/12/98
 protection from Antichrist (Jesus) — 4/2/98
 to fight evil (Jesus) — 6/25/98
Sacred Heart Feast
 open arms to His love (Jesus) — 6/19/98
sacrilegious Communion
 do not violate gifts (Jesus) — 6/14/98
saints
 call on for help (Jesus) — 6/11/98
 defended the Church (Jesus) — 6/30/98
 examples in life (Jesus) — 5/26/98
 models for conversion (Jesus) — 6/29/98
salvation
 Jesus is personal savior (Jesus) — 4/21/98
Satan
 hate for mankind (Jesus) — 5/19/98
 hates man, wants death (Jesus) — 4/17/98
Satanic power
 to gain riches (Jesus) — 5/7/98
satellites
 controlled by (Jesus) — 4/30/98
 natural disruptions (Jesus) — 5/26/98
schism
 battle of good and evil (Jesus) — 6/22/98
 choose John Paul or antipope (Jesus) — 4/17/98
 decision of priests, laity (Jesus) — 6/15/98
 underground Church (Jesus) — 5/22/98
 underground Mass (Jesus) — 4/16/98
 underground Masses (Jesus) — 4/7/98
Second Coming
 Mary is preparing for (Mary) — 4/23/98
 role of Mary & Holy Spirit in (Jesus) — 4/12/98

# More Messages from God through John Leary

If you would like to take advantage of more precious words from Jesus and Mary and apply them to your lives, read the first three volumes of messages and visions given to us through John's special gift. Each book contains a full year of daily messages and visions. As Jesus and Mary said in volume IV:

*Listen to My words of warning, and you will be ready to share in the beauty of the Second Coming.* Jesus 7/4/96

*I will work miracles of conversion on those who read these books with an open mind.* Jesus 9/5/96

*Prepare for the Great Tribulation and the Era of Peace*

**Volume I -** *Messages received from July 1993 to June 1994*
 ISBN# 1-882972-69-4 256pp. - $7.95

**Volume II -** *Messages received from July 1994 to June 1995*
 ISBN# 1-882972-72-4 352pp. - $8.95

**Volume III -** *Messages received from July 1995 to July 10, 1996*
 ISBN# 1-882972-77-5 384pp. - $8.95

**Volume IV -** *Messages received from July 11, 1996 to Sept. 30, 1996*
 ISBN# 1-882972-91-0 104pp. - $2.95

**Volume V -** *Messages received from Oct. 1, 1996 to Dec. 31, 1996*
 ISBN# 1-882972-97-X 120pp. - $2.95

**Volume VI -** *Messages received from Jan. 1, 1997 to Mar. 31, 1997*
 ISBN# 1-57918-002-7 112pp. - $2.95

**Volume VII -** *Messages received from April 1, 1997 to June 30, 1997*
 ISBN# 1-57918-010-8 112pp. - $2.95

**Volume VIII -** *Messages received from July 1, 1997 to September 30, 1997*
 ISBN# 1-57918-053-1 128pp. - $3.95

**Volume IX -** *Messages received from Oct. 1, 1997 to Dec. 30, 1997*
 ISBN# 1-57918-066-3 168pp. - $3.95

**Volume X -** *Messages received from Jan. 1, 1998 to Mar. 30, 1997*
 ISBN# 1-57918-073-6 128pp. - $3.95